# Clearly Broken

## The Voice of a Heroin Addict

Jay Devin Koch

Clearly Broken: The Voice of a Heroin Addict
Published by Austin Brothers Publishing, Fort Worth,
Texas

www.abpbooks.com

ISBN 978-0-9996328-5-7

Printed in the United States of America
2018 -- First Edition

A portion of the proceeds from this book go to the
Freedom Court in Lubbock, Texas to assist those
struggling with addiciton.

Dedicated
to the
memory and legacy
of our
beloved son,
Jay Devin Koch.


"If I got just one last night to live again
I'd make God proud and I'd face my sin
The opportunity seemed to be at my fingertips
But yet again, I bumbled and let it slip."

# *Contents*

**Good Advice**

## Recovery

**The Final Battle**

# *Prologue*

The Lubbock County Community Corrections Facility/Court Residential Treatment Center (CRTC) opened its doors in March 1993, offering residential substance abuse and dependency services to adult males on community supervision. Currently, the CRTC facilitates four diverse treatment programs with the ability to house 164 offenders. The goals of the CRTC are to prevent relapse, prevent recidivism, and to promote living a meaningful and responsible life through treatment for criminal conduct and substance use.

The CRTC offers education on criminal conduct, substance use, prosocial behaviors, and coping skills. The core curriculum focuses on education and coping skills for both substance use and criminal thinking. The CRTC offers up to 30 different classes and groups to provide individualized treatment for each resident. Through this education and guidance, the CRTC promotes a crime-free life of recovery.

In 2009 it was decided that a formal court-supervised aftercare program was needed for some of the probationers who had completed the CRTC. Many of the CRTC graduates have a tough time adjusting from a lockdown facility with no availability of drugs back to the real world of less structure and old friends and playgrounds. Out of this need and due to much valuable input and discussion from all of the stakeholders, a unique specialty problem-solving court was created.

I am honored to serve as the presiding judge over this re-entry opportunity that is now called "Freedom Court."

We have come to learn that addiction is a medical/physical disorder and addiction has to be addressed differently than the conventional way of locking up and warehousing addicts. The old way of dealing with this issue was very ineffective and extremely expensive in many ways. Something had to change, and Freedom Court is part of that change.

A Freedom Court team, made up of probation officers, a prosecutor, a criminal defense attorney, counselors, and a certified peace officer meets once a week to determine an appropriate plan and response to each individual probationer according to their needs and as a response to their decisions made since the last court session. Each case is staffed, and a recommendation is made to the Judge who ultimately makes the decision as to how to handle each probationer so that maximum success can be obtained. The team and the Judge share and display a real concern for each probationer. Positive re-enforcement is one of the keys to success in Freedom Court in addition to an accurate and robust drug testing protocol. The Judge builds a trusting relationship with the probationer by assessing appropriate, fair, and timely sanctions and rewards. Freedom Court consists of three phases, and on the average, a probationer will graduate after being in Freedom Court for 12 to 18 months. Of course, some don't make it and are handled in a more conventional manner.

At present, only about one-fourth of the graduates of CRTC are placed in Freedom Court. Lack of resources prevents placement of all of the CRTC graduates in the program. [Jay Koch was not staffed as one of those probationers to be ordered into Freedom Court.]

Learning of Jay's story and reading his dynamic poetry motivates me even more to help others that are in the same position as Jay was before his untimely death. Good has already come out of his death, and that goodness will continue for a long time.

A special fund has been established to assist the Freedom Court team in utilizing positive motivation by way of financial awards and incentives. These take the form of bus passes, fees for taking the GED, housing assistance, job training, gift cards for food and gas and other basic necessities.

A portion of the sales of this book will be donated to Lubbock County Specialty Court Foundation to assist the Freedom Court.

**Hon. William C. Sowder**
**State District Judge, Lubbock, Texas**

# The Voice of Addiction

Our son, Jay Devin Koch, was born six weeks prematurely on March 3, 1987. It seems he was as eager to enter this world as he was to leave it some thirty years later. This proved to be an inauspicious beginning to his life. As do many premature infants, Jay faced numerous physical challenges during the first weeks of his life–breathing via a ventilator, a renal system that shut down, and heart surgery at three days old. We saw what a warrior spirit Jay possessed as he survived each of these challenges to grow into a beautiful little boy with a kind and loving heart.

His only remaining physical condition was asthma which was also to play a role in his eventual demise. Had we known what lay ahead for our son, would we have fought so valiantly at birth to keep him on this earth? Absolutely, without any doubt.

Jay grew into a charming and intelligent child. He was a "low maintenance" infant and toddler–quick to laugh, content to play alone in his crib, and eager to face bedtime after a full day. Although he remained small in stature, Jay enjoyed good health other than asthma. He was doggedly teased by his older brother, but Jay found Paul to be the ultimate source of fun and delight as any two brothers might. When caught mid-caper, Jay would be the first to admit "Paul did it" just as quickly as Paul admitted, "Jay did it." Sibling rivalry ran rampant in our household but the boys, with opposing personalities, enjoyed each other's company while growing up.

Paul and Jay looked very much alike, but I joked with them that God had used a different box of crayons for each of them. Paul has an olive complexion, dark brown hair, and dark eyes with chiseled features while Jay had auburn hair, fair complexion with freckles, and green eyes. Paul had more chiseled masculine features while Jay had softer features.

Paul and Jay also differed greatly in personality–Jay developed into a more sensitive soul who was interested in sports and military history–especially the American Civil War and the Texas revolution. If there was a game show featuring these topics, he would have been the grand champion as he memorized vast sums of knowledge from reading about those time periods. One of Jay's favorite past times as a child was playing "dress up," not as a fictional superhero, but as a figure from history. Jay also developed a love for writing at an early age–primarily because he was upset there were few "history" books made for young readers. It is his love of writing that made this book possible. In the last year of his life, Jay explained that what he could not say in a therapy session, he could write in his poetry, giving a voice to the specter of addiction.

Over the last 13 years, my husband Danny and I have, unfortunately, learned firsthand about drug addiction as Jay began abusing alcohol and drugs in his teens. You may be thinking, "Danny and June must have been horrible parents," but in truth, we were loving and supportive parents, and we were involved in our son's life. Jay grew up in safe neighborhoods and attended good schools where he was an A student with no behavior issues until his senior year in high school. These are no longer safe barriers that ensure our children are protected from the epidemic of drug abuse in our country. Addiction can and will happen to any family.

In the beginning, Danny and I did not see addiction as a disease but rather a choice made by our son, a poor judgment call, a crime, or a sin. We were still in the "Just say no" frame of mind. Only later did our son's suffering show us the true nature of addiction as a disease–an all-encompassing, dreadful, mental health disease that destroys everything in its path. No one in their right mind

would choose this disease. No one grows up want-
ing to be a junkie.

Jay points out in his poetry that he had oth-
er life plans–he wanted to be a soldier, a husband,
and a father. More than anything else, he wanted
to serve his country in the military, but he learned
as a teenager that the military would not accept
him because of the heart surgery he had as an
infant. Jay's childhood dream was crushed, and
I don't believe he was ever able to replace that
dream with something else. You could say he saw
himself as a failure before he even began life, so
he chose to never begin. Several times he started
college, achieved the Dean's List his first semester,
but then dropped out the next semester. From his
writings, we understand he greatly feared grow-
ing up and assuming responsibility, so he ran
away from both through drug use.

Through this book, I want to introduce to
you an authentic voice of drug addiction by, what
better way, than to bring you the words of a drug
addict. Over the years, Jay filled four notebooks
with drafts of his poetry which he entitled, "Di-
ary of a Heroin Addict" –it's the brutally honest
voice of addiction like I had never heard before.
Danny and I believe Jay's writings speak not only
to those struggling with drug or alcohol addiction
but also help families understand what their ad-
dicted or recovering family member is experienc-
ing. We have already shared some of these poems
with clients at the local parole offices, and their

clients have let us know that it moves them and they relate to Jay's stories.

From his poetry, we know Jay's addiction was all-consuming, and he was well aware that it could take his life. In fact, he wrote of his desire to finally bring an end to his pain by dying the way he had lived–as a drug addict. How painful is it for a parent to read that all their beloved son yearned for was an end to his own life? You can only imagine unless you have watched someone you love commit a slow suicide for 13 years. Only God can explain why one addict survives while another does not, but as parents, we struggle daily with feelings of guilt and shame that we could not save our son from his addictions, even though we are reassured that only an addict can save himself. We are comforted by Jay's autobiography in which he wrote that he felt very close to his parents, especially in sobriety. Unfortunately, addiction is a place where a parent's love cannot go.

During the last month of his life, after Jay had been released from a Court-ordered rehab program called County Residential Treatment Center (CRTC), he began finalizing and compiling his poetry into book form. Danny and I believe Jay knew he just might not make it through recovery and he wanted to leave this book of poetry for others–for those who struggle with addiction in their lives and, perhaps, as a roadmap back from grief for his parents. We are so grateful for Jay, his love, his writing, and for the 30 years we were gifted with

him as our son–despite his heartbreaking strug-
gles with drug addiction.

Jay wrote that he began experimenting with
marijuana at age 14, but confesses in his autobi-
ography that he did not like it very much. He de-
scribes his descent into addiction:

> The loss of my first love at age 18 fol-
> lowed by my giving up my hobby of Civil
> War re-enacting affected me negatively and
> my drug use began very soon after. By nine-
> teen years old I was full-blown drug addict.
> During my junior and senior years of high
> school, I drank heavily with a high school
> friend. Then I began using pills, mostly hy-
> drocodone, with my brother. Although my
> brother and I did not get along when we were
> growing up, drugs became a way we could
> bond with each other. Over the years since
> then, I have tried every mainstream drug,
> many synthetic drugs and I've been addicted
> to at least 3 or 4 of them. Before I came here
> (CRTC) I was addicted to heroin with a minor
> in methamphetamines. ...I wish I could say
> using left no physical scars on my body, but
> such is not the case. Internally I am not sure
> how much damage I've done especially since
> I used needles exposing myself to bloodborne
> pathogens. I have experienced withdrawals,
> especially from opiates, heroin, and synthet-

*ic marijuana. I've also experienced blackouts from drinking and using drugs.*

We have come to realize that Jay's mental health played a large part in his addiction. His poetry describes the depression that plagued him as failed relationships, regret, despair, and a desire to stop the pain that his life had become. Many of the recovering addicts we have spoken with tell us this message is how they felt also.

During Jay's teen years and twenties, Danny and I sought professional help for him many times with no success. Jay would often "check himself out" of a rehab program because it was a voluntary commitment. I am convinced today that a comprehensive mental health treatment policy and program in our country could save many people who struggle with this disease. Just look at what they have been able to do in Lubbock County through the CRTC and Judge Sowder's Freedom Court. (see Prologue)

There were occasions in the past when we had to order Jay to leave our home due to his drug usage, and he spent a good portion of that time living on the streets or with friends. We tried to be loving and supportive, but we also tried hard love when necessary. Unfortunately, on his journey through addiction, Jay stayed with people who served as *enablers* and allowed Jay to use drugs in their homes during the times we evicted him from our home for the same reason. I know they meant well, but we had to extract Jay from those situations as we fought to bring him back to sobriety.

Although we supported Jay financially in the early years of his addiction, in 2016 after he broke a window to enter our home while we were away to steal electronics and blank checks which he later forged, we faced the painful decision to file criminal charges against our son. We knew Jay was out-of-control at that time, and we felt it was his only chance to survive. This is how Judge Sowder and the CRTC came into our lives.

After being arrested on a felony charge of possession and burglary, Jay went through withdrawal and suicide watch in the Lubbock County Jail before being transferred to the CRTC. This is an excellent program that Jay could not walk out of as he had at previous rehab centers and he received the counseling he needed, including cognitive behavioral therapy.

His poetry written during his time at the CRTC shows significant changes in his outlook on life. Jay's writings began to reflect that he was ready to embrace sobriety and begin the life he had never experienced before due to drug addiction.

"I've found a new path under my feet
Marching away from another retreat
Shadows float away on the breeze
My soul thaws from under a freeze.

Love is patiently waiting just up ahead
Phantoms of words I left unsaid.
Bridges rebuilt and are made whole
Eyes locked onto a worthy goal."

Toward the end of his time there, the CRTC staff helped Jay obtain a job at a local restaurant, but unfortunately, drug trafficking and drug use are prevalent in the restaurant business. Jay told me that an employee at the restaurant was tempting him to buy cocaine. After 15 months, Jay received his 1-year sobriety coin from Judge Sowder and was released from CRTC. Rather than sending Jay to a local "Sober House" to live, Danny and I agreed to allow Jay to return to live in our home, but in hindsight, this was probably not the best idea.

Jay seemed to make positive strides in maintaining his job for one month after graduation before he quit due to a dispute over work hours at the restaurant. In a matter of hours, Jay bought Cocaine from the co-worker at the restaurant, and he relapsed on Sunday, November 12, 2017. We counseled Jay to follow procedure, and he did self-report his relapse to his probation officer. Danny and I foolishly assumed that this was the end of that relapse episode and that Jay would continue on with his sobriety.

As I had many times before, I asked the eternal question of "Why." Two days later he wrote a poem in response: "Why, Jay?" He explains he relapsed because he wanted a "last dance with the devil."

Six days after Jay relapsed, on November 19th, Jay asked me around 4:00 pm for a ride to a local discount store to meet some sober friends for the evening. We learned from reading his text messages the next day that he went to the discount store to meet a drug dealer and buy heroin. I will forever feel guilty that I gave my son a ride to his death without realizing what we were doing.

Can you imagine, the garden center of a public store is a place where drug deals take place daily? We later found the last poem he wrote shortly before he went to purchase heroin. Perhaps the hardest thing for us about the poem, "Internal Strife" is that we were in the next room while he wrote it, but Jay never came to us or ask for help.

Several hours later, Danny gave Jay a ride home, and he was suspicious that Jay was high on something, but he was not certain. Jay came home and told me good night and showed me a new pillow he had purchased at the discount store stating he would sleep well that night because of that pillow. Since then I have wondered if he meant something more profound in this statement as he did have severe insomnia, as do many addicts. Jay had a glass of juice, told his dad good night, and went to his room.

On Monday, November 20th, Danny and I were surprised that Jay did not get up to have coffee with us as he usually did. He loved coffee but we assumed Jay was tired so we let him sleep in. I noticed throughout the day that Jay was not calling or texting me as he normally did. He would often call or text throughout the day just to chat or tell me what was on his mind. Danny works from home, and he called later that morning to say that Jay was still not up and he was concerned, but he had to travel out-of-town for a meeting that after-noon.

By 5:00 I knew something was definitely wrong because I still had not been able to reach Jay by phone, so I rushed home from work. I literally threw my purse and coat on the breakfast table and ran to Jay's bedroom toward the back of our home. I opened the door and immediate-ly saw Jay crumpled on the floor of his bedroom next to his bed. Apparently, he had sat up on the edge of his bed, put on his bedroom slippers, and then fell face down onto the floor.

The first responders told me that Jay died in-stantly because he made no effort to protect him-self from the fall. You can imagine how this sight impacted me–I was so terrified that I immediately began running away down the hallway to get away from that sight. I stopped cold when the thought occurred to me that he had been alone when he died, and I knew I didn't want him to be alone any longer, so I returned to his room.

With indescribable pain in my heart, I knelt beside Jay and touched his neck and right shoulder. He was as cold and as hard as a stone. I called 911 from his room, and I only remember telling the operator that I just could not understand how my son could be gone. She asked me if I wanted to start CPR and I told her it would not be useful because he was obviously deceased. In order to calm me, she asked me to kneel down beside Jay again and describe to her in detail what I saw as she sent emergency responders.

I then called Danny, and while crying I tried to tell him that Jay was gone but Danny kept asking me where had Jay gone and what did I mean? I don't think he could accept the sad truth either. But it was true–our beautiful, funny, charming, golden boy was indeed gone.

The official cause of Jay's death was "Toxic effects of heroin" combined with a history of asthma. From his writings, I understand that he died of hopelessness, despair, and depression. He simply could not face starting over in life one more time. As he wrote, he could not wage another "battle in an unending war."

I hope Jay's words will help others understand the disease of drug addiction and know that it is not a disease that only affects "bad" people who make bad choices. It is a disease of people who have no hope left in their lives, and they treat their pain by self-medicating. Initially, a young person may try drugs for the high or the rush, but Jay once told me that you soon begin taking the drugs just so you can feel "normal." Jay saw drugs as the only way he could forget about his past–the terrible things he did to obtain drugs and his wrecked relationships, and he could also forget how he had squandered his future.

I also hope that the message of this book that the face of addiction looks just like our sons, daughters, brothers, and sisters will touch your hearts. Jay's words written at the end of "Mortal" give me great hope and peace–I know I'll see my son again someday.

To those who are struggling with their recovery from addiction and reading this book, I hope you found resolve and the strength of a warrior to continue your battle. Please don't live like you are planning to die–but live as if you are going to live–for a long time.

# *Addiction*

# Broken

Are you as clearly broken as I am?
Tell me true and I'll give a damn.
Trust me, its okay if you are shattered
Ripped and torn, dirty and tattered.


Beneath your surface I see the cracks
Do you, like me, hate hearing the facts?
Soon you'll reach the point of no return
Then you will break before you burn


Your voice it is cracking just like glass
With your destruction the pain will pass.
I've been where you stand times before
Don't do as I and beg for more.


Do you have a sutured heart like me?
Through your flesh and blood I see
You're melting like heroin on a spoon
Those stitches will ultimately fail soon.


The canyons in your soul are growing wider
You're bloody and bruised like a fighter
Nothing said repairs what's been undone
From all the damage you cannot run.


Your weary body is fast becoming a shell
Even the blindest of us are able to tell
Yet still you grasp for what was lost
Your self-destruction will be the final cost.

# Bullets

I couldn't answer any of their questions
God knows I refused all the suggestions
It may have been easier to face a firing squad
Surely bullets break bones better than God.

A question mark has become a crooked smile
Supported on bleached bones stacked in a pile
Buried alive by questions breaking the dirt
Reaped and sown in the grave for my hurt.

I answered in mutters with adverted eyes
How to respond when confronted with lies
The blindfold was placed, day turned dark
Pray hard the bullets find their mark.

How many times did I sit before a judge?
Every guilty verdict tasted like a grudge
Under God's sun I underwent interrogation
Always feeling the jury's harsh condemnation.

It was I who tied my hands behind my back
As if fingers could ward off the bullets' attack.
All the lies made the answers hardest to find
Now the questions are ringing loudly in my mind.

No reply for those who deserve one the most
Truthful answers were as transparent as a ghost
I yearned like a fiend for the triggers pull
A final release from feeling like a damn fool.

# My Lover My Heroin

Hell yeah, here we go! I scored some dope
That reoccurring devil in which I put my hope
Heart pounding, its back to the house I race
I relish the feel of blood rushing to my face.

The silver spoon is shaking in my weary hand
This hobby of Hell ain't close to what I planned
Now, I sit in a messy, cluttered room all alone
In erotic anticipation I sit there still as a stone.

My arm is tied off and the needle is ready
Lord above guide my hand and keep it steady
My breath goes shallow as my eyes flutter close
Pray tell, did I do too much of the drug I chose?

Where the point pricked remains some blood
Through my veins the black heroin does flood
High above, God, broken hearted, sees me use
Does he damn me at all for every single abuse?

Is it just me, or am I really floating far, far away?
Nothing tethers me here to life's constant dismay
Finally, I'm embraced in chemical heaven's bliss
Another victim I am of the syringe's sweet kiss.

# Darkness

Can you taste this present darkness?
It consumes mind, body and soul.
Feel the edge's lethal sharpness
Don't let the dark swallow you whole.

Darkness will soon become complete
I know the fight you wage, you'll lose
All you'll ever know now is defeat.
Will the results only serve to confuse?

Feel the icy grip of amicable dark
You can't run be it slow or fast.
The darkness hunts you like a shark
Ready to consume your entire past.

It's funny that you're trying to hide
The dark can see through all the light
No one is left in whom you can confide
Again I say, you've fallen from sight.

Darkness was made from all your stress
You've nurtured it as if it was a child
How you can't clean up your own mess
The ramifications are so far from mild.

Can you spell out your coming doom?
There on the horizon it's trying to wait.
For forgiveness there is no more room
Don't be judged by the hands of fate.

# Deja True

Life is but a dark and sinister déjà vu
It's like a joke that cuts inside of you
Every day loops and plays on repeat
Come what may nothing is ever complete.

Time is a laughing beast that likes to mock
Its cage is the failing, broken old clock.
Every second is but a clone of the one before.
Long ago the minutes gave up keeping score.

Nothing really changes between weeks and years
This sinking ship flounders among the tears.
Yesterday is the hellish same as tomorrow
Like a banker's client we beg to borrow.

I feel like I've been living in a joke
Wandering and lost in heavy clouds of smoke.
No exit has yet been made to be found
Here among a mundane life I have drowned.

I've been blind to the days being the same
Wasting time is how I've spread the blame
Life has become a repetitive type of Hell
No peace exists for the Devil to sell.

What do I do to make time move on?
I'm tired of being déjà vu's reluctant pawn
Something will eventually sever this chain
Until then, I walk closer to being insane.

# Dying Ain't Living

I resigned myself to living a twisted existence
Sadly enough I didn't offer much resistance
The life of a junkie appealed in some way to me.
A junkie's death I prayed would set me free.

How strange to live life searching only for your death
It's not normal to up and forsake every breath.
I guess with dope's influence that's all I wanted.
My better self was a ghost that left me haunted.

There are folks I know who are living just to die
Because the dope steals the right we have to cry.
Drugs took my sight and they made me a slave
The whole time all I yearned for was my grave.

I thought all I needed was love and acceptance
All God expected was to hear sincere repentance.
Death taunted me by always hanging out so near.
Its dark presence was one I never did fear.

Live by the drugs die by the drugs was my hope.
Every syringe and shot only tightened the rope.
My slipknot heroin broke more than just a vein.
The tar-like substance was enough to make me insane.

I resigned myself to die the way I chose to live.
Mercy wasn't expected because mercy I could not give.
Dying is never easy and living can sure be tough,
But everything is when the needle just isn't enough.

# Here nor There

Yeah it's clear to me my dear why I'm here
Here is where we've never really been
My afterlife was born of strife and by the knife
Here is where we will meet again.

I heard a prayer said on a dare to skip a scare
There is the same as it never was
On my knees I've sent up pleas hoping my God sees
There is not what tomorrow does.

What's absurd in the promise I heard in every word
Here is the same as every yesterday
I made a vow not thinking of now or much less how
Here is the bill the past will pay.

Where's the chance for another dance, spare me a glance
There is where I met my reject
Just another strike counted to like while pugging the dike
There is going to know its neglect.

I've confessed I passed the test by my very best
Here is the stuff made of dreams
Leave this all alone at home frightened to the bone
Here is everything heard in screams.

Everything was a loss stuck on a cross up for a toss
There is out of the window
Anything to gain was such a pain falling rain
There is lurking in the shadow.

# Insomnia

I'm spinning wheels and chasing sleep
I have no luck with counting sheep
Into my mind I can't help but creep.

All around me are thundering snores
The insomnia is leaking from my pores
I can't hide behind any dreamy doors.

Sometimes I'll endure an endless night
My red rimmed eyes will blur my sight
The sandman and I are looking to fight

Pray tell, will you feel sorry for me?
Know this is a seldom paid fee
Usually the moon will let me be.

Tonight it hurts to even close my eyes
I gave up after one too many tries
Now I'm praying that tomorrow dies.

The light is blinding from the moon
Her sister, Sun, faded far too soon
Lured to rest by the starlight's tune.

This time there's no drugs I can swallow
No pill to choke down to keep me hollow
Nothing will cause sweet relief to follow.

# "Hope and I"

I gave up on Hope and gave her away
I don't want to face that life today
It's much easier living in negativity
I almost enjoy this sick depravity

Watch my Hope get put up on a shelf
There she'll stay until I find myself
It's a travesty if I do take her down
She'll adorn me like a broken crown

Days burn out and melt on into years
Months die and lay in rest with fears
This Hope is the same all of the time
Different lies cover the same crime

My Hope died in a moment of despair
I knew its demise was another scare
Hope is a Lazarus like state of mind
It is always there for us all to find

I tried to give Hope away for free
Like giving new legs to an amputee
Alas, she clings to me like bad luck
I stand in awe that Hope has stuck

The affair we have is so love - hate
I'm cheating on Hope with lusty Fate
Don't tell anyone or Hell will be born
Hell has nothing like my Hope's scorn

I'm a bad boy for how I treat my Hope
I keep her dangling here by this rope
She's on my life's roller coaster ride
What can I do to turn away and hide?

Don't do as I do, learn from my life
Forsake Despair and all of her strife
Cherish your Hope and treat her well
Losing her is a guaranteed death knell

Hope and I are such an odd couple
I'm so stubborn where she is supple
We don't always agree but she wins
I get angry and go reassess my sins

She is always around me in all I do
In good or bad, if I'm happy or blue
Maybe I should stop fighting back
Quit working up courage to attack

# Life's Battlefield

I've walked over my share of fields of fire
Those footsteps left tracks and caused me to tire
No man's land is scarred by explosions and death
Flame and smoke makes it hard to catch my breath.

Nothing is able to live long on life's battlefields
Death has control over all and its power he wields
The body may live but the soul itself can die.
Fear turns into adrenaline that gets me high.

I've fought alone and surrounded by my friends
With help or not, the fight turns to an end
The field is littered with broken, torn casualties
My constant reminder of my mortal frailties.

Amidst the smoky hell I struggle and fight
Looking through a tunnel searching for the light
With every foe cut down a dozen more appear
Turning forward I fall back from facing my fear.

Bugles and drums sound over the din of the fray
I give thanks that I've made it through the day
Tomorrow will bring another fight much the same
"Ground Hog Day" is the title of this old game.

By night I lick my wounds and toss and turn
Nightmares relieve the fight and my memories burn
I wake with a start, my weapon in my hand
But there is no way to best my demons and stand.

# La Aguja

The done is gone the needle dull
Left laughing is Death Head's skull
I'm haunted by fallacies I remember
There's nothing left except surrender.

Rusted scars adorn my pale flesh
Ash and dust still try to mesh
Veins stitch together and heal
My heart leaves how to feel.

Hands of time are covered in blood.
While legs of fate stick in the mud
This story is something so sinister
It scares God's bravest minister.

Memories I live with every day
What a damned tragic toll to pay
No words exist to make amends
Apologies linger for run off friends.

So this is the world I endure
I've given up hope for a cure
This goes deeper than self-will
God knows there is no magic pill

The needle's sting carries a price
The drug's release cannot suffice
This addiction, she'll last forever
From her grasp I cannot sever.

# Left by the Lost

I stumble around as the lonely, blind, lost
Here I'm a debtor unable to bear this cost.
This time around there's a huge heavy fine
Only this go I'm accepting responsibility as mine.

The light in my hand a while back went dead
Now where's the exit sign hanging in my head?
Infinite darkness is all that is surrounding me
I'm bound in its clutches fighting to be free.

There's no pre-made path I am trying to follow
A travel guide's directions barely even ring hollow
This map's usefulness has long ago expired
God help me this searching has made me tired.

Corridors twist and wind as if I'm in a maze
I got lost and left behind in all my ways
The dead ends never seem able to materialize
Off the walls echo the lost forlorn soul's cries.

There's no more S.O.S. messages for me to send
My calls for aid have all died on the wind
I fear I'm forgotten and unable to be found
Every sigh is exactly how hopelessness will sound.

Life's maze has been long devoid of any kind of fun
My legs are worn down from trying so hard to run
I can't climb over nor burrow under those walls
What's left to do but roam along the vacant halls?

# Lost Cause

Exactly what have I been fighting for?
Is it God or the Devil who's keeping score?
I believe in a cause I made profound
Lying to myself over doctrine unsound.

I fought for a cause damned to fail
Petty ideals drove me through Hell
My convictions were so very easy to steal
Yet, what was sacred was it even real?

I waged wars I had no right fighting
Always in the chaos I would be delighting
The storm clouds quickly gathered overhead
My resolve would fade until it was dead.

A demon named Resentment is who I fought
That angel of Hell deflected every shot
We fought in combat that's hand to hand
In the end, only one would stand.

Behind him stood Shame, Hate, Guilt
All demons I alone had built.
Such an onslaught kept me insane
It was always wave after wave of pain.

Man versus Demon can be hard to win
Seldom is victory for the race of men
I'm tired of hanging onto a lost cause
As worn out as can be from my flaws.

# The Body of ...

See the vein beneath the skin
Blow it out again.
Blue lines beneath flesh so pale
Condemn it all to Hell.

Feel the pink, puckered scar tissue
The needle was an issue.
Marks linger as punctuation marks
They glow in the dark.

Hear the blood as its flowing fast
The heroin was a blast
Highways of crimson cross my heart
The dope broke me apart.

Touch the nerves that have frayed
A smile so very dismayed
Pain shoots from bottom to top
Please, God, make it stop.

Believe that the mind knows it all
The brain takes the fall
Memories and thoughts move and flow
So the past tends to go.

My body has taken a real beating
Destruction was repeating
More than just bones can break
So much is at stake.

# The Night

Every night wound up being exactly the same
I had the stars down pat in repeat memories
Resisting the day's appearance became a game
There was nothing new to see in any of my reveries.

I struggled hard to keep up pace with the stars
What kind of race was I really trying to run?
The night time always helped to etch more scars
To me my nocturnal identity was half the fun.

The night's darkness seemed to consume my heart
It beat me up, black and blue and up and down
Some kind of hellish demon tried to tear me apart
While light from the moon ignited our every frown.

The vaunted night gave me a safe place to hide
Time flew by so fast between the sun and moon
With the setting sun my nightmare finally died
Yet the rising of the sun always came too soon.

When the day came, the sun would take the stage
Like a vampire I could not bear to face the day
I felt as if I was a beast locked up in a cage
My soul burned to ashes when hit by the sun's rays.

# Lunatic's Lament

I don't want to remember, no, not anymore.
Not sure if anything flushes this shit away,
You see I figured memories would fade
I'm left here missing someone to adore
This is the amount I have to pay
My sins are the foundation that's laid.

From who I am there's nowhere to run
I've draped my mirror in long black thread
I won't face myself in image or in reality
Playing this hide and seek ain't fun
Looking in closets full of my past's deed
Trying to remember skeletons with no ability.

The Devil is greedy and demands his dues
Levying fines on the broken backs of men
Purses are barren like the hangman's very soul
No debit or credit for a mortal to lose
I've long ago paid in full the wages of sin
An indebted slave no longer with any control.

Reckon this time the joke's falling on me
Funny how I hear no one else laughing.
Watch the crazy man convulse in humor's fit
Caged in bedlam. For six pence, you can see
This lunatic's lament is far beyond baffling
I must be hilariously insane mired in a pit.

# The Night's End

Sitting in a room in the dead of night
A spoon, a lighter, a needle made it right.
Biding time in hopes of some absolution
Take a pledge for sobriety's revolution.

Waiting in a place I figured was home
Watching the reaper come for the sown
The clock ticked by for all eternity
So I shot up the CCs of my remedy.

Anticipating the dawn's bright rising sun
Thinking daybreak I could some way out run
I took another hit just to kill the hour
The euphoria lied about my mortal power.

Pacing the floor until the carpet was raw
In my mind I misconstrued God's law
Crushed up pills plunged into my old vein
At least for another hour I'd be free of pain.

Crossing through doors into yet another room
Hearing the noisy silence of my impending doom
Load another rig with my bitter brown medicine
For a minute I enjoy a chemical laced grin.

Retracing my steps and it is back to the start
The needle has over-amped my now fragile heart
How frustrating this dirty spoon that refuses to bend
So for dawn I wait, loathing the night's end.

# Corpuscular

The night is such a sweet purgatory
Etched in time and draped in glory.
In the darkness sins can hide
Where the moonlight always lied.

Did I live to resent the dawn?
Becoming night's celebrated pawn
With the sunset I came alive
Among the stars I learned to thrive.

My nocturnal life became a habit
Down the hole I pursued the rabbit.
I chased the dope with shots of hate
Caring less and less about my fate.

The night was but a sweet enemy
A twelve hour fix for a remedy.
Just a tale written in my bloody ink
In crimson letters the truth will sink.

Tomorrow's cares perished with the sun
From yesterday's demons I couldn't run
Only for the darkness did I care
While the light I blamed as unfair.

Against the clock I waged open war
Quickly forgetting what I fought for
Always the night would end too soon
So I wept bitter tears over the moon.

# Welcome Home

Welcome home to all you've never been shown
Now bow down before the rickety old throne
Your false God remains here finally all alone.

Did you really think you called every shot?
I too reckoned I could never be bought.
Look how wrong it was to fight all for naught.

Welcome home to the place that's made of walls
I'll watch you wander listless through the halls
See the legends of all your history's old falls.

How did you falsely claim you were oh, so great,
I never beat the bell cuz I was already late
You too will advance beyond the mention of fate.

Welcome home to an unimagined kind of hell
Do you wager you know Heaven far too well?
No, you've fallen under the evil's new spell.

I can't help but to ask what is left to show
You have the bill with the balance we all owe.
Still the darkness keeps what you'll never know.

Welcome home just in time to watch tomorrow die
The last thing you'll hear will be a heavy sigh
Will your false God be left behind asking, "Why?"

It wasn't okay to think you were the only one right
Nothing I did could be hidden from my God's sight.
Today we rally, regroup and prepare for a new fight.

# The Door

Let me exist in this cold, barren, lonely hotel room
White washed walls painted over in shades of gloom
Some cracks in the ceiling mirror my heart's state
The knock on the door locked tight comes too late.

I can't get up from this scratchy, cheap old bed
Concrete hard pillows cradle my heavily held head
These sickly stained sheets wrap me in their arms
No pounding on the door will stop the coming harm.

Yes, I know I've forced myself to be left alone
What kind of king am I sitting on a fake throne?
Only the furniture in this room bows to my rule
Kicking in the flimsy door won't save this damn fool.

The phone in this place has been ripped from its cord
I can't make a call for help to a savior called "Lord"
My noisy silence echoes and fades all around me
A battering ram against the door won't set me free.

Staggering then crawling I seek out the room's mirror
Expecting what? That somehow I would see clearer?
I hold myself up at the edge of the dirty sink
Making it through the door won't re-establish any link.

Rescue me from this sheetrock and plaster made hell
The air that I choke on in here is fast going stale
Hands to my throat I cough and gasp for more air
Please hurry and close the door; I can't stand the glare.

# Too Far Gone

Don't sit there and tell me everything you see
As far as I'm concerned you don't understand.
How do you sit there and declare your empathy?
You must be sick to think you can offer a hand.

If I wanted help I'm sure I would ask
But here you come again ready to play the game
You're blind to expectations in line with this task
Is that what tells me your help is equal to zero?

I may be crazy, but friend, you are a fool
What can you offer that I don't already have?
In my sight you're no better than a tool
But what the hell, go ahead, give it a stab.

Will you blame me if you can't make me right?
I'm telling you that the odds are way too high
You've gone awry by picking the wrong fight.
Down the road you'll be regretting this try.

I won't stop you, but know that you've been warned
This fiasco is starting, but watch, it's going to evolve
Run or stay it's your own choice, but you will be torn
My problems are only my own and up to me to solve.

Don't hesitate a beat but come on with it
I'm waiting to be saved as you so richly claim.
Your efforts are laughable so let's stop this shit
This wild child is too far gone for you to tame.

# Man Made Monster

Let it be said that this monster must be fed
Hungry and hopeless it lurks beneath your bed
Chaos and fear helps keep the monster so near
Feed the beast daily and you'll tether it here.

So what do you expect when we all starve regret?
The monster's memory is long; it won't forget
Its sharpened claws rip and shred a man's flaws
This beast will never be bound by our human laws.

Our monsters we create and make them great
This ravenous being is one we don't appreciate
My beast is borne of my scars and dying stars
Insatiable and hunger like the ancient god, Mars.

Every whip that is cracking is found to be lacking
Nothing keeps this monster from resolutely attacking
There's no place to hide by any savior's side
Like a mechanical bull you're on for the ride.

Your beast you can't defy so why do you try?
The monster grows stronger with your every lie
So hard you've fought and you've lost a lot
Yet adamant you are that the beast can be caught.

Whatever story we tell the creature comes from Hell
The consistency of this evil will never come to fail.
Has the day come and gone for you to move on?
Does the monster yet remain to witness the dawn?

# What's Good is Gone

In life the good can surely come undone.
I've seen it happen like the day's rising sun.
No, I suppose good's death is far from right,
Who am I to define what is worth a good fight.

So, all good things must come to an end
It ain't right that God alone can mend
I struggled thinking I had some control
But what good remained fled from my soul.

Do you think that good and hope remain?
All I've seen is the lying that serves to maim.
I broke the engine that fueled the good
Because a fool always does what one should.

The bad reigns supreme in the good's vacant place
Breaking open the bad is a task hard to face.
Then what kind of test is going to be taken
Will it leave you all alone, so far forsaken?

All I once believed as good long ago it fled
I never saw the tombstone declaring it dead.
The funeral was held but I was never invited
Between the good and the bad I am divided.

Like a house divided the good is unable to stand
That's the result of a plan once described as grand.
Now I see that good has come to be undone
All that's left for me to say is, "Run, run, run."

# Crushing Cross

Burdened under this cross's crush
All for craving a fix and a rush
I can't carry a Christian's lumber
The high lulls me to false slumber.

I never planned to live this way
Somewhere I forfeited my final say
Every step has been a hellish task
Hydrating from Satan's hip flask.

My standard is best torn and tattered
Flying high over a heart shattered
"Carry On!" That's the cry I hear
In disembodied voices drawing near

My shoulders were fractured long ago
Trudging along like a snail so slow
I feel my back start to give out
The angels hear my strangled shout

How much weight can a man carry?
The scales register numbers scary
This load feels like it weighs a ton
I yearn for the day this is done

My knees buckle and then I fall
Like an airplane that's in a stall
With a thump my body meets ground
Flesh hitting dirt the only sound.

# Night's Revolving Door

So many nights painted in sadness
Fatally sickened by all my madness
I ignored how the heavens mourned
Focusing only on what I scorned.

The demons refused to let me sleep
Fruitlessly I kept trying to reap
Evil kept me locked in my sheets
Playing while delivering new defeats.

The man in the moon laughing hard
I struggle to gain another yard
Seeing double I aimed for a star
The bullet didn't make it far.

I fought for all that I hated
Sailing a voyage always ill-fated
Evil began to revolve around me
In the darkness it is hard to see.

I ran in circles every single night
Stuck on insanity's perilous plight
Gaining nothing except what is lost
My heart was layered with frost.

Riding a ride with eternal admittance
The day's dawn always in the distance
Did the sun ever bring the end?
On its mercy I refused to depend.

# A Place of Darkness

In that dark place died humor
A victim of my addiction's tumor
That's when I heard angel's cry
Accompanied by the sounds of a lie.

I was overcome with melancholy
Coming in waves, volley after volley
The darkness came in and took over
Forbidding a try at being sober.

Where I went I pray no man goes
Living at the bottom with my lows
I wanted to climb out of that hole
But by then I had given up my soul.

I was a bully, the ultimate dick,
Looking back will make me sick.
I acted like a spoiled little kid
Still can't grasp the shit I did.

That place was like an empty tomb
A fetus growing inside Satan's womb
The light could never penetrate
Into the depths where evil congregates.

I was lost deep inside and confused
A self-inflicted victim to the abused.
Today I have no excuse
I alone chose to be a recluse.

# At One Point (Then)

At one point I gave up on hope
Opting to live for and die by dope.
Of that life I want no small part
All it gave me was a broken heart

At one point I forgot how to care
My eyes locked in a thousand yard stare.
False love made me so unbearable
False gods make existing terrible.

At one point I lived with lying
The whole time I kept on dying
Truth became a high priced joke
Hard to purchase when you're broke.

At one point I forget every value
Looking for another victim to screw.
I was a dead saint for every crime
The biggest thief of history's time.

At one point I gave up on me
Unwilling to face my evil's spree
I didn't care about what I was
Destroying all, saying, "I can because!"

At one point God's love was forsaken
Of how badly I was then mistaken
Walking away from Him who loves all
Going instead for a junkie's fall.

# Body Etchings

I tried to etch "Love" on my arm
Through scars borne of the needle's harm
Jaded love is all that is left
The remains of my heart's last theft.

Love was not a permanent tattoo
The ink dried before it bled through
A single word causes me to reminisce
I forget the hell and not the bliss.

I couldn't stop love as it bled
No tourniquet could save the dead
Thriving on the ink's crimson flow
Picking the scab to let love grow.

Jilted ink lies below the skin
A tattooed list of all of my sin
I refuse to claim this as art
Behold tattooed stitches on my heart.

The needle cauterized my every vein
Giving me the rush from disdain
I became a most cynical critic
Not owing up to how I was sick.

I tried etching "Hate" on my knuckles
Smiling through all the false chuckles.
My body has been bled and bruised
With this end game I am not amused.

# For Sale

I have a broken empire for sale
The asking price, no, I won't tell
The ruins still smolder and smoke
My coffers have all come up broke.

Truly, you get just what you see
All this for a con-man's honest fee
The walls fell with a loud rumble
Helpless, I could only watch it crumble.

Alone stand gates once built strong
Let me tell you how it all went wrong
Come with me I'll be your tour guide
Don't wander off or leave my side.

Broken streets wind just like a maze
Haunting voices cry out for better days.
Yes, I built this all by my hand
No blueprints remain of all I planned.

I fancied myself a great architect
But you can't build on slabs of regret
This imperial lie is all I ever knew
For once the truth I'll say to you.

No surprise that I met a Roman's fate
I was fighting my pride a second too late
Now, if you're ready, here's the price
Will you take the chance and roll the dice?

# Heroin Holocaust

I lived it, my own personal holocaust
Some kind of a private final solution
Numbers don't do justice to all that I lost
In the end life was sickened by pollution.

I watched as souls were turned to ash
The fire churned but couldn't keep pace
Broken spirits were thrown out like trash
I destroyed it all hoping to save face.

Locked up and numbered like so many cattle
Tattooed numbers took away every name
I saw me die alone in my life's old battle
In the crematorium evaporated my shame.

The ghetto I built only pre-empted Hell
I packed my bags and I sold my heart.
Locked in a room that was my prison cell
Waiting for the soldiers to tear me apart.

A needle in my arm, a yellow star on my chest
A symbol for all the blind masses to see
To eradicate my curse I tried my best
As I waited for someone to save me.

I lived, this man-made hot conflagration
Bullets and gas can only kill some time
So I remain to build up a ghostly congregation
As I burn the trail leading to my crime.

# Numbing Coldness

I feel so cold and so numb
My inner works are fouled by gum
I'm as frigid as Minnesota's lakes
Not yet immune to life's heartaches.

Touch me and your skin will freeze
Does this curse set you at ease?
This isn't something I have flaunted.
Closets full of ghosts keep me haunted.

"You can't feel numbness," they say
But they don't know me that way.
What I feel is for me alone
With feelings that provoke a groan.

You see me wear a fake smile
It can't be adjusted by a dial.
Is it not enough to know my place?
Reeling from all the demons I face.

Is numbness just a state of mind?
The cold permeates everything I find
What fire is made to keep me warm?
What shelter exists when I face a storm?

Yes, I feel so numb and so cold
A repeating story waits to be told
None of this was part of my plan
Yet, I have no control as I am a man.

# The Devil's Serenade

I've had enough of the Devil's serenade
On the breeze his melody won't fade
A choir of demons will always join in
The chorus a haunting refrain of sin.

I've danced a dance that seems eternal
All to a noisy racket that is so infernal
The orchestra has played down to the bone
Every melody is composed of a ghostly moan.

I know the words to this most evil hymn
Singing for help perched on a breaking limb
The syllables catch deep down inside my throat
A final song played on a sinking boat.

This song used to be set on Hell's repeat
All the while every stanza was incomplete
There is no shuffle on Satan's playlist
No matter what, no verse can go unmissed.

I nodded my head in time with the tune
All while praying for it to end soon
Through my mind swam the hope of grace
As broken arms reach up towards God's face.

The Devil's serenade gets stuck in your head
It drives you to wishing you were dead
Escaping is hard once you're in its grip
From sanity's hold it causes you to slip.

# *Good Advice*

# An Adversary in my Memory

That memory just took away my breath
It left me feeling lost, as cold as death
She waltzed across my mind by chance
I wanted to join her for one more dance.

It happened as quickly as any vaccine shot
So fast the memory that could not be caught
Yet, it lingered long enough to sting
Nothing was left except a hollow ring.

My mind's eye stopped me in my tracks
I can't lie anymore about the facts
Memories are all I have left now
Remembering is now to what I bow.

Reckon I like pain all to the extreme
Never thought she'd become a dream
Yes, it hurts to ponder all that was
I want memories that will leave a buzz.

She flirts with my mind that much more
Her eternal presence I fail to ignore
With thoughts akin to playing cat and mouse
Eventually, only one will remain to rule the house.

It's not that I want to erase my mind
No, I don't want thoughts I can't find
I'd like to be content with all my memories
Seems that could be one of my safe remedies.

# Chill Pill

Something is telling me just to wait
Is this the vaunted voice of Fate?
Her trembling words I used to hate.

Patience is the weakest of my virtue
I can't handle a wait, that's true
Impatience is the curse that grew.

At this point all I have is time.
Truly, patience is worth many a dime
Forcing my hand would be a crime.

I'm used to rushing in like a fool
Guess I used to think the risk was cool.
What was I but true love's tool?

Instant gratification was always my way
Always would I refuse any sort of delay.
This time I think its come what may.

What's wrong with taking another raincheck?
Hell, waiting is no big deal on this long trek.
I'm curious to see what's next up on deck.

Some folks say, "Take a chill pill!"
It's wrong to rush around for a thrill
So now it seems it's time I will kill.

# Where Were You, God?

Where were you, God, through it all?
Never did you catch me at any fall.
Didn't you see me hit life's wall?
Hell, did you even hear my call?

Where were you, God, in every bad choice.
Tell me, did you ignore my voice?
Were my cries merely background noise?
Was I just one of your broken toys?

Where were you, God, when it went wrong?
Did you happily just watch or tag along?
True, I refused to sing your song
But the chorus was far too long.

Where were you, God, as I broke apart
Couldn't you tell me I wasn't so smart?
You, the one who knows every heart
Why wait for me to have a new start?

Where was I, son, but right by your side
From my love and mercy you did hide
Truly son, it was you alone who lied
It was you that I suffered and died.

Where was I? Busy carrying you
Look inside, you know it's true
I'll always be here to see you through
And yes, I make old into new.

Where was I? This you ask me
Who do you think set you free?
I have always been and always will be
Open your healing heart and you will see

Where was I? All along I've been here
I have taken note of your every fear
Yes, I've even bottled up every tear.
Through thick and thin, I'm always near.

# Depression

Look inside the recesses of my mind
I can guess as to what you'll find
Places darkened by excessive shadows
Not as lovely as Fiddler's Greens meadows.

There's a battle raging on in my brain
It's like a song's never ending refrain
Over and over these legions continue to fight
Take a peek inside and it will fill your sight.

Depression is a demon I fight every day
Sometimes I fear the illness holds sway
There's a dark veil just behind my eyes
Looking through the veil spells my demise.

Yes, I've tried to pretend it doesn't exist
At times I've fought back trying to resist.
Ignoring the monster did nary a thing
It fed the beast, making a stronger being.

Can anyone direct me where I go from here?
Is there a map that's drawn crystal clear?
You can't point out the best direction to take
Nor can you cure me for Heaven's sake.

# God's Name

It's very unwise to think God's a fool
Just as it is to use Him like he's a tool.
At his feet I used to lay all of my blame
Because my life has dissolved into a game.

Yes, I'm the fool who screams at the sky
Cursing God and demanding to know why.
Why, oh God, did you make me this way?
Is there no response He has left he can say?

His silence was the most unacceptable answer
It spread through me like malignant cancer
Do you judge me as if that's your right?
How? You've never seen life through my sight.

I thought I was punished for an old sin
God was making me hurt time and again
Accusing Him has kept us far apart
All He wants is to stitch up my broken heart.

It's hard knowing He has been betrayed
Forgiveness I've sought every time I've prayed
I never knew God's heart can even break
The sound of his pain is a tough one to take.

No purpose is served by labeling God as cold
That old belief is one that kept me on a hold.
Now I believe He and I can agree on hope
And that we can get off this slippery slope.

# Hate

Hate's a bitter pill for some to take
With a taste closer to heartache
Swallow it down with dirty water
Then feel Hell's flames get hotter.

I take so much I overdose
This medication makes me morose
Hate takes all of my last energy
No doctor provides me a remedy.

Hate tries to consume a weary heart
As love and lives are torn apart
So easy it is not to offer a fight
I'm overcome by this evil's might.

Oh sure, we all try hard to resist
But the point thereof I've missed
What man can ward off his hate?
Dancing along to the tune of fate.

With hate our loves goes astray
Every strong moral we will betray
I've only traded one for the other
Keeping Satan close like a brother.

Hate's a foul pill I swallow
With no chaser trying to follow
Inside it breeds dark resentment
Feeding off the dying resentment.

# "I"

I won't go quietly into the night
No, it shan't happen again
I won't go down without a fight.

I can't stand up for very long
Yes, I won't win this time
I can't prove to anyone who's wrong.

I don't fret that I haven't a prayer
Yet, I can't give up and quit
I don't think the battle will be fair.

I mustn't throw my arms up in surrender
No, they'll show me no mercy
I mustn't forget who is the defender.

I won't go along with this insanity
Yes, this choice is my own
I won't give in to human vanity.

I can't try to draw a battle plan
Yet, it'll come down to this
I can't pray for any other man.

I don't commit to my old false belief
No, it always seemed to fail
I don't revel in my past's stale grief.

I mustn't lose faith in what is dear
Yes, the future is my beacon
I mustn't lose sight of what is clear.

# Let Go

I've struggled learning to let go
Folks claim I like to be in the know.
Far too often I feel the need for control
As if such is nourishment for my soul.

The fate of my life is in God's hands.
He is generous in honoring my demands,
But I have to surrender to His will.
Am I willing to forfeit deceptive skill?

I fail to have charge of much in life
Did that by-and-large create my strife?
Too often I fight against surrender
Thought I could fake it as a pretender.

Like Custer fighting in his last stand
I hold tight to as much as I can
Perhaps this is all just a matter of pride
The old man is fading, he's gone and died.

Can't rightly say if it's right to hold on
When everything familiar to us is gone.
At what point do we cry, "I can't do this"
We cross the line between reality and wish.

Holding on hurts in ways I do not know
For all my trouble I have nothing to show
I white-knuckle my past far too much
If I don't let go, I'll soon be out of touch.

# Wrong or Right

It was all wrong but it felt so right
Thriving in a sick maniac's delight
I embraced everything that's sinister
Every time a shot I would administer.

Against myself I committed high treason
I was lost in a hurricane's stormy season
Around me swirled winds of heroin and meth
Hoping the storm would become my death.

Everything I did was far beyond wrong
I took a hostage and she went along
Let me accept that I alone am to blame
Such is the result of my life's deadly game.

I gambled against the worst odds laid
Trust and love awoke only to be betrayed.
The end result no person could estimate
Who knew I could become all that I hate.

Now I'm worn out from rolling the dice
My veins are thawing from the frigid ice
I finally see that to gain one must lose
What was lost is exactly the evil I abuse.

I am right to see the wrong that I chose
From here it gets better I truly do suppose.
I don't have another try at being sober
And getting high ain't a four-leaf clover.

# Double Trouble

I found my share of trouble
Running around living on the double
What is here left that I can show?
The best of me I managed to overthrow.

Yes, I lived as no man ever should
Wrecking destruction on all that's good
My deceit became black as night
Honest was driven from my sight.

I did more than just break the law
On a pedestal I put up every flaw
Misery loved my company the most
Tripping me up as I chased a ghost.

Now, I get to pay for my past
I know this too will not last
The cost goes deeper than money
So much so that this ain't funny.

To right the wrongs will take time
I accept this from all the crime
There is no rushing into all this
Because this target is hard to miss.

Consequences will help make a man
When before this I turned and ran
Sadly doing the right thing is new
Yet for once it's something I will do.

# Hurricane Jay

Like a twister in a trailer park
I easily hit every single mark
Nothing and no one was left standing
As I came in for a crash landing.

No man's will would have stopped me
Only God alone could have set me free
I was a hurricane made in Hell
Everything, everyone I destroyed well.

My storm was far from predicted
And in no way was I restricted.
The world I knew was fair game
Another tornado no one could tame.

The destruction wrought cannot be missed
Scores of casualties adorn the list
Man or woman, I took them both
But from that chaos comes new growth

Winds subside, the sky becomes blue
I trashed everything I held dear
Hopefully this final storm will cease
How foreign it is to know this peace.

Now is the time to pick up the remains.
What a chance to clear away the stains
A broken life I now must mend
So here I began at the end.

# Let Sleeping Dogs Lie

One day I'll learn to leave something alone
To date that boundary remains unknown
For reasons unclear I keep pushing life harder
Forgotten at the bottom of a hole I dug larger.

I expect an answer to change from bad to good
Nothing I ever touch goes as it really should
My power over matters is actually very small
Yet I expect favor however the chips fall.

At times I push too hard and life pushes back
Then I retreat in the face of such an attack
That's what happens when I try to force a hand
My way of doing things is hard to understand.

Usually there's a price to pay when I push a boundary
The balance I get on the bill is extraordinary
My mind, heart, and soul are the ones to pay the fee
I fork over the cash with eyes too blind to see.

This isn't the first time I have tortured myself this way
I can take the best of times and weave a bad day
Be it a phone call, a text, or an old fashion word
All are deadly enough to maim, to kill and to hurt.

With age I hope to learn to accept life as it is
Acceptance is a key factor in if, or how I find bliss
The past is exactly that and what's done is done
I should let everything go with the setting sun.

# Memories in Whispers

It's easy to recall all the good times
Making the bad memories harder to find
We all like to share a good-time story
Doesn't matter if it's funny or if it's gory.

Most of my life was spent ignoring the bad
That worked pretty well in keeping me glad.
I blocked out the consequences of actions
Such faulty thinking held back any corrections.

I can focus on the good all my life long
The memories generally write a pretty song
Such biased thinking never did me a favor
Because when shit would hit the fan I'd waiver.

Sure it's great to remember all the laughing joy
They remind me I once was a carefree little boy
Smiles plaster my face with the good of yesteryear
That keeps me from dwelling on all the fears.

Now I see merit in remembering when I fell
They're just as much a part of the story I tell.
I actually like remembering the pain and hate
Often enough I recall the bad a little too late.

What's the point of memories that haunt?
They are not unlike the victories we flaunt
We show off the grand while we shun the poor
Ignoring the raven as it cries, "Never more?"

# My Afflictions

Well I never thought I would be this sick
Plagued by two diseases I cannot lick.
There are treatments to make it through
They are part of the things I have to do.

My first struggle came up as depression
Piggy-backed immediately by addiction
It felt much like a double sucker punch
No one gave me a warning, I had not a hunch.

Depression I can treat with talking and pills
No medication can fight addiction's thrills.
Addiction is arrested by Steps I walk
Still it lurks like a lioness that stalks.

With time's progress narcotics took me over
Self-medication I preferred over being sober.
I dealt with the sadness by getting high
Never thought medications were worth a try.

The drugs just made my depression worse
Both diseases had me yearning for a hearse
A couple of times I opted for suicide
Thankfully my fears stopped me at petrified.

Now I'm glad I made it through every day
That was not always something I used to say.
Today I have more hope than ever before
Such hope are points added to my score.

# My Pearls of Wisdom

What would I say to myself back at eighteen?
Cause at thirty my hindsight is worth being seen
Twelve years has made its mark in every way
There's a lot I'd be willing to up and say

It would only be right to offer up a warning
That's something I now see as worth learning
"Take it easy, pal," that's the line I'd use
There's so much more in life you could lose.

Don't be so stupid and get back into school
One day you'll regret skipping out like a fool
Finish what you start, it'll help make you a man
Always trust in God and trust in His holy plan.

Run away from drugs and the many fake friends
Don't' give up in adversity as it will always end
Be your own person not what other folks build
Grow your faith strong as it'll be your shield.

Love others and never take them for granted.
That's a good seed of logic I never planted
Women are special and they're more than a prize
Respect them always, kid, never feed them lies.

Find what you love doing and then give it your all
Never be afraid to step out and risk taking a fall
When you don't get your way, don't throw a fit
Bite your tongue and never just up and quit.

Chase your dreams and set some realistic goals
You'd be surprised as to what's in your control.
Failure happens to us all so cut yourself some slack
Take a chance and be willing to go on the attack.

Forgive yourself and others for whatever was done
Don't be the one to blame for not having fun
Live life without holding on to every little regret
Learn from your past and try not to just forget.

Friend, make good choices no matter what they cost
Always pay attention to the line before it's crossed
Respect other's views because you're not always right
Don't' argue with friends or go off looking for a fight.

Finally, live every day as if you know it's your last
Don't fear the future or yearn for your past
Live for the sake of living, don't live just to die.
And know that real men are never afraid to cry.

# A Poem for the Addict

It is so hard living for a hit
Doing your damnedest to stay lit.
Every day you're down on your luck
Not seeing what's keeping you stuck.

You learn to live hoping to die
Immune to how you make God cry
As an addict you learn to loose
You quickly forfeit the right to choose.

Just one more shot and one last score
Getting high is all you live for
You know help is in the distance
Why put up so much resistance?

The lifestyle keeps you on the gallows
Treading water in a pool so shallow
As hands reach out from all directions
You push back the notion of corrections

I've been there and it ain't no joke
The Devil steals and leaves you broke
He laughs louder as you sink lower
In a suicide that kills even slower.

Stop playing this Russian roulette
There's better things on which to bet
Don't die before you finally see
That God's light will set you free.

# Chuck

I saw an old friend today
He's living that same old way
Counting minutes 'til "beer-o-clock"
Still bound up in chains and lock.

Beyond "Hello" we didn't say much
Guess our worlds are out of touch
Yes, my heart goes out to him
He's trudging a path dark and grim.

I can't judge because I've been there.
Playing a game stuck on the same square.
In common we'll have our memories
I'll see him again in my reveries.

I saw an old friend on the bus
There he goes doing what he does
Was I wrong to not offer my hand?
I should've done more to help him stand.

Strange how we sat so far apart
Yet I felt a tug at my heart
We may as well been across an ocean
Riding the waves on the bus' motion.

I can't help him before I fix me
That truth of life I finally see
So I give him to God in a prayer
Asking for relief from his despair.

# On and Gone

What does it take for a person to move on?
I feel like a piece of me is dead and gone.
Here I sit and grieve holding onto the pain
It's become an umbrella against the rain.

I want to let go of everything and be done.
Still I find myself trapped and unable to run.
My heart has somehow been turned and betrayed
I feel like the flesh from my bones has been flayed.

My heart tells me this is all only temporary
Thank God this road won't end at a cemetery.
Time ticking by is what will heal these wounds.
How do I lose myself in the sands of time's shores?

My mind screams at the clock to pick up the pace
I want to get over this and finish up the race.
Every day can be a struggle with a heavy toll.
Sometimes it's with the punches you got to roll.

Nothing can be done to help speed up the clock
I'm linked to the past by a hefty chain and lock
I best hold on and make it through every day
Truly I know within that there's no other way.

I have to hunker down and take this in stride
The pain is out there and I know I can't hide.
I may as well go ahead and accept this fate;
It's okay to hurt and feel either joy or hate.

# On Any Given Day

It feels like a very good day to be alive
I believe I'm beginning to finally thrive
The wind on my face is the sweetest kiss
And the color of the sky is what I've missed.

Every morning I wake up I choose my kind of day
If it's good or bad, either one, it's my way
During some days it can get rough at any time
Letting fear rule the day ain't worth a dime.

My situation isn't hopeless like it has been before
Now I'm feeling hope and I want much more.
Every day I live now is closer to happiness.
I no longer try to live for other folk's forgiveness.

A growing faith in God gives me a firm foundation
He's taught me not to fear imagined condemnation
I put my life in His hands daily through prayer
His love makes every cross much lighter to bear.

I feel confident I can tackle whatever may come
Problems will arise that's just the equation's sum
This way of living beats just existing
I'm getting close to ending my resisting.

# This Too Shall Pass

We all fear the loss of someone we love
Some think it punishment from God above
Nothing could be further from the truth though
I think it's another way that His love will show.

My wish is to take away some of your pain
Friend to friend, I know it's pouring like rain.
Just know you don't walk down this path alone
Hold on and salvation is going to be shown.

Answers in the dark are often hard to find
So put the pursuit thereof out of your mind
Truth is acceptance and the key to all our issues
It's normal to mourn and need a tissue.

Brother, my heart reaches out to you.
I want to help, give me something to do.
I don't have much to offer just to be frank
But my empathy is pretty high in rank.

The cliché goes that: "This too shall pass."
I know it seems like this hell is gonna last
Have faith in the process and what is coming
From God's plan or fate, there is no running.

# Martyr Mania

Here I am just another broken martyr
This is the life I chose to make harder
I picked a fight for my own demise
My ammunition was lots of force fed lies.

Flaws, like nails, hung me on my cross
The crown on my head counted as a loss.
Other people's sins became daily crucifixion
I didn't discount my incorrect conviction.

The suffering became my cherished liability
I was always afraid to take on responsibility
Any miracles wrought here were not by my hand
How'd I convince myself I was taking a stand?

I was the fake hero so full of zero power
So convinced that any evil I could devour
Wars I waged were but self-made illusions
The first one who would jump to conclusions.

Now, I'm so afraid to look into the mirror
Full of fog I half believe I see clearer
The ghost looking back surely can't be me
I turn the lights out but still I can see.

What kind of martyr did I hope to become?
All my fears equaled up to too great a sum
No, I'm far from perfect, this I now accept
I'm sacrificed myself to all of my regret.

# *Regrets*

# August 21, 2017

So here I sit with a sober
I take my past and look it over.
Eleven years of the darkest hell
Boy, have I a story to tell.

Things didn't go the way I planned
That's the result of my forcing my hand
I fought everyone and everything
Deafened ears can't hear angels sing.

I used to want much more than this
A wife, a family, and eternal bliss
With a career and a college degree
Instead I went on a foolish spree.

It all went wrong because I couldn't cope
Desperate, in pain, I found the dope.
In ones and twos I swallowed the pills
Paying out for illegitimate thrills.

Chasing the dragon became my new game
Like a wounded horse I came up lame
The law failed to scare me enough
I was able to call the court's bluff.

I continued on and in misery I wallowed
The poorest role models I followed
A broken dream for a soldier's chance
That sent me back without a glance.

I drank deeply of the acid rain
The drugs easily deadened pain
At a dare I moved back home
There for a bit I wasn't alone.

Further down, I felt myself go
Nothing more than a fool on show
I broke more laws than I can count
There's no defense I hope to mount.

I did things I claimed I never would
Tragedy followed me as it should
I failed to act like a good man
In the end I was evil's biggest fan.

A year later and I'm starting over
From here I know what to do
I'll pick up the pieces and carry on
No, my life is not yet too far gone.

One battle's over but the war rages
Every day I get to take it in stages
I'm okay with having this disease
I'm not okay with living on my knees.

I know now the price I have paid
I know now where burdens are laid
I know now the cross I must carry
I know now that regrets I can bury.

# Balance Due: Deceit

I sold it all for a bitter taste
A deceitful kingdom laid to waste
The thorny crown fell through my hands
Sharing the fate of my best laid plans.

What I needed was what I wanted
Spirits remained to keep me haunted
Warped priorities replaced all I knew
Stealing my desire to see it through.

I ignored the hefty price expected
While responsibilities I neglected
Thinking I was a man among men
Pure as snow unblemished by sin.

So auction off an unsavory chance
False surprise burdens every glance
Behind the walls of my debtor's prison
The fog masks the heart that's risen

Nothing is easy and it is never free
My angels hold me before I flee
Life's a razor thin balancing beam
It keeps me gasping for a scream.

I want a refund with no receipt
To balance this ledger of deceit
Yesterday's demons negotiate on lies
Hateful guardians of the sacred prize.

# Fairy Tales

Has your life been a fairy tale?
A happy ending meant to fail
How much went according to plan
It died with the touch of my hand.

Show me the ruins of your empire
Rome's glory is all you desire
Yet the Barbarians remain at the gate
Has this demise come far too late?

Kiss the princess hoping she'll awake
The Prince Charming I can't fake
Sleeping Beauty is in Death's grasp
A withered rose yet still she clasps.

My castle crumbles into the moat
The dust in the air remains to gloat
King Arthur has forsaken Camelot
To pull the sword he took a shot.

What do you ask the mirror on the wall?
Did you leave your slipper at the ball?
My stories have all run together
Locked in the past and trapped forever.

What fairy tale do you claim to live?
Is there any joy in it to give?
Hopefully you will have a happy ending
Happily ever after can be so demanding

# A Haunting Remains

There must be things inside me I've left unsaid
Whatever they are, they are driving me out of my head
I'm inflicted with a wound that can't ever be bled
This monster has been lurking underneath my bed.

My soul and my tongue seem to be beyond paralyzed
I'm unable to speak from a list I've itemized
The horrors inside have caused me to be traumatized
This shell of a little boy once too often criticized.

An unknown seed was planted down in my chest
It's sprouting and growing as it feeds off my best
The nagging it delivers is harder than any test
Uncertainty ringing within is denying me my rest.

What is this phantom that haunts me day by day?
Is it another beast in a long life I have yet to pay?
Nothing has yet to satisfy it no matter what I say
This ghost is in my heart where it continues to lay.

How do I unshackle myself from what's holding on?
What's left in me refuses to get up and get gone.
This ethereal remnant is using me just like a pawn
It leaves me starving for the light shed by dawn.

This festering cancer wants to burst from inside me
Apparently I'm not able to set this demon free
For reasons I fear, this feeling won't let me be
There's something holding me back that I can't see.

What has yet to be said I can't seem to speak?
Am I sealed up tight and unable to leak?
The words rest on my tongue which I can't tweak
Am I some kind of blind and mute exiled freak?

There's this business unfinished that's left me reeling
Now I'm being chased and can't shake this feeling
My happiness and sanity are what this evil is stealing
What's being taken makes it hard to seek the healing.

I guess I'm not purged yet of all of my regret
No longer can I turn a blind eye hoping I'll forget
This is a game I've lost on every one of my bets
I feel like a soldier whose objectives weren't met.

# Ghost of Years Past

"Hello, son, tell me where should I now begin?
Can you single out the greatest of all your sin?
A flashback's whim, that's where we will start
But be warned: put a guard around your heart."

Are you my Christmas past time-traveling ghost?
Can I wake up from the sleep I enjoy the most?
Hear me out; this journey isn't what I choose
I feel that doing this leaves me a lot to lose.

"Sorry, friend, but it's back to the beginning
From there we'll see you as you start sinning.
Hold on as we go back almost twelve years
When we arrive, we'll get drunk on your tears."

What tears? In over a decade not one's been shed
Truly I wonder if that means my emotions are dead
Twelve years it is and that's quite a lot to handle
Don't be surprised by all of my life's scandals.

"Well, look at you go with a needle in your arm
That's a quick way to bring yourself harm.
Life tried to scare you with a brush with death
But you didn't listen in the time it took to draw breath."

Hold on, was the heroin alone really the sinful worst?
Surely you know there are more parts to my curse
Yes, I see the needle go in and blood come out
Can I wake myself up with a desperate shout?

"Not yet friend, but look there's love at the door
How badly you wanted her and nothing more.
Boy, you sure reeled her in like a fish
It made you feel swell getting your wish."


Yeah, but we met in a loud, dark chaotic bar
That was a sign that we wouldn't make it far.
At first I was a part-time sober, part-time gentleman
Honestly treating her like royalty was my only plan.


"So selfish, boy, you wanted both of the two:
Drugs and love combined meant the most to you.
Now here's the night you put dope in her veins
Turning a blind eye to demonstrate taking the reins."


You got it all wrong here! I really did her a favor
She asked me to do it and so she excused my behavior
We claimed to love each other and that's all it was
I mean come on, spirit, isn't that what true love does?


"Does true love allow a man to strike whom he loves?
The sound of the hit echoed up to your God above.
Please tell me, my man, just what were you thinking?
Don't you dare blame her or her heavy drinking."


Look, I admit there isn't any kind of an excuse
No man should ever put someone through that abuse.
Now I'm riddled with shame for what's done is done
Please, stop here so I may awake before the sun.

"I'm sorry but there's more to see in this dream
Nothing will rouse you, not even your scream.
What did you expect from living in a nightmare?
Your actions were crazier than any past dare."


Oh, so I did some stupid stuff when I was young
Now my past is the very noose from which I'm hung.
So for the sake of my sanity, let's get this over with
The sooner the better to get me out of this myth.


"As you wish, let's move on to your overdose
See yourself lying there barely even comatose.
She pumped your chest to keep your heart going
You never said, 'Thanks for keeping my blood flowing.'"


It's just another sin for which we know I'll burn
Now please, from this torment won't you let me turn?
I was wrong, so wrong, yes, I see that so clearly
Already I've lost everything I once held dearly.


"There's more to see before I bid you good-bye.
Let's move on to the truth and how you would lie
You expected forgiveness with no thought otherwise
How shocked you were when confronted by your lies."


Hey, not everything was a lie that I spoke to her
Yet I can't defend how little I told her the truth.
How wrong to not even fear any of the repercussions.
Hell, phantom genie, my lies weren't up for discussion.

"You thought you could use drugs and be in control.
Did you not see the drugs took over your soul?
By getting her addicted you kept the balance right
Opting for the chaos you kept within sight."

For the love of God, will this torture ever end?
I give up on any argument I can use to defend
Truth is, my demon, that yes, we chose to sever
My broken heart is reeling from another false forever.

"We're almost there now that she has moved on
How does that make you feel knowing she's gone?
By the look on your face it hurts like hell
Is this what you deserve? Only time will tell."

Leave me here in this deepening dark gloom
I can't accept just yet that I've made my doom
What must I do to get you to leave me alone?
I reckon you've done your job with what you've shown.

"We're all finished here, looking into your past
Don't worry about the pain, it shouldn't last.
Hopefully you've learned from what was taught
Do you really want to relive the nights you fought?"

That dream woke me up and it made me feel
The implications were heavy enough to make me reel.
It's fine that I'm going to hurt a while
Even the deepest pain won't steal my smile.

# Fate or Destiny

I'm twisted up in the hands of fate
They're wringing out the things I hate
Leaving me here in front of Hell's gate
I stand in line preparing to be late.

Fate treats me like I'm a toy
Time is the worst kind of decoy
Trust me this is not what I enjoy
What type of a defense can I deploy?

Destiny has only the strangest of flavor
It is nothing near what I will savor
But come what may I have yet to waiver
This may be the taste of a new savior.

What is this that keeps life pre planned,
Is this a god that hears every demand?
This sorcerer of time will offer no hand
Destiny and Fate they will forever stand.

God's fortune teller is upon who we rely
She utters no words and nary a cry
Is it fortunate Destiny will never lie?
No man alone will cause Fate to die.

I hope you understand all of destiny
God knows she's the one I'll never see
Fate keeps me waiting for all of eternity
Her time is rationed and far from free.

# Judge, Jury and Executioner

The jury is coming back with a verdict
Waiting for it to be read makes me sick
"Guilty!" the foreman reads his voice clear
Something's broke inside as I shed not a tear.

After all the evil I did this is what I get
Karma is taking a toll for all my messed up shit
The price I pay for the hurt I caused
To become much more aware of all my flaws.

I fear the coming sentence that is impending
This self-made torture is never ending
You see I don't enjoy this newest reality
It makes me feel much like a sad casualty.

The judge in this court is ruled by my hate
A double edged sword with which I tempt fate
What will he decide to do with this evil saint?
The coming decision makes me feel faint.

Mercy is something I know I don't deserve
And there's no image I have left to preserve.
I'm hoping for the best, but expecting the worst
Go ahead, load me up in my broken down hearse.

Like a shotgun blast I hear the gavel sound
Something tells me my justice has been found.
I'll hang my head and accept this hell.
Please remember this man did die well.

# Reminders Without Blinders

I see this is what's called a gentle reminder
I don't want to behold this using blinders
Not in any way is this to be considered painless
For having to go through this I am not blameless.

Moving pictures flash before me in the slowest motion
Words of the past reappear in a loud commotion
Tears sling my eyes like water that's held by a dam
This time I can't fake the memories by living a sham.

My weary heart races like the gilded chariots of long ago
Being here again is what goes with the current's flow
For reasons not faced I'm being reminded again
This is another repercussion for my well known sin.

Being reminded of my last night was a great shot
On its back were memories of battles I fought
Victories are hollow in comparison to my defeats
That's all I ever knew, with my life set to repeat.

For so long these reminders I've tried to avoid
The lurking presence helped make me paranoid
It took twelve years for me to face my bitter past
My demons were patiently waiting for me en masse.

I faced the fight and came out okay to my surprise
Reminded of the evil I almost let be my demise
The question till remains, "Where do I go from here?"
Time alone will answer me in ways that are clear.

# Light the Fuse

Can you feel this burning regret?
It glow like the last cigarette.
The vapors tell me I don't belong,
Yet pride claims, "You're not wrong."

Around my heart the fuse is lit
It's strangling off my "give a shit."
I'm bracing for the next explosion
While my soul suffers from erosion.

No water can snuff the flame
I'm burning alive in life's game
Inside me sits a powder keg
For relief I've tried so to beg.

Here's my wages for a day's work
Satisfaction can't erase this smirk.
Every day adds yet more explosives
A quick remedy that is corrosive.

I find I'm bereft of desire
My past lags cold on a funeral pyre
Strike a match light the kindling
Once stout reserves now are dwindling.

I ask should I stay or should I go?
Is the answer something I know?
There's no outrunning time's fuse
Born to run, too stubborn to lose.

# Soul

A soul can be a hard thing to steal
Evil always comes as a night time thief.
I promise you the threat is very real
Losing your soul will only bring grief.

I have stolen souls and had my own taken
At those times I never shed even a tear
Now I begin to feel my regret awaken
My soul was left behind wrapped up in fear.

What right did I have to steal a soul?
I held it ransom at the end of a gun
How was it okay to assume I had control?
My hostage was trapped unable to run.

I sold my soul for a very low ball price
The price I got wasn't close to fair
Living indebted to evil isn't living nice
An empty inside, like mine, can cause a scare.

Stolen or stealing — both end the same way
Plenty of victims but never ever a winner
Both parties are going to have a price to pay
They will both answer on the knees of a sinner.

A soul is something we all should treasure
God delights in what we have deep inside
The value thereof no man can ever measure
Our soul is the "self" where we can hide.

# Time Immortal

Time has begun the bad habit of dragging by
Nothing is quite as scary as asking it, "Why?"
No matter what's done, the clock will not fly
So desecrate the face hoping the minutes will die.

The clock's numerals are my old slashing scars
Every minute spent hurtles you to the bars
Nothing stops time as it travels beyond Mars
It carries on far beyond our burning stars.

The hands of time reach out to stop the day
That's how it happens, no there's no other way
The clock will win no matter what we'll say
Time immortal is the piper every man will pay.

I wish I had the power to speed up time fast
Now every second seems to slow down and last
Where's the separation between future and past
The clock is a bomb begging to make a blast.

Why does it feel like the clock's laughing in my face
I'm running like a snail locked in a sprinter's race
How damn hard it is to match time's frantic pace
Suffocating the innocent in a beauty queen's lace.

Time, it's the one constant thing I fear won't end
As a youth we all richly claim it is our friend
Yet with age we hope on time we'll never depend.
The clock is the wound no one can ever mend.

# An Empire Sold

Here's my broken empire's price, friend
Thank you for helping this travesty end.
For this you must give all that you are
Such a sacrifice will take you only so far.

Sign here by the "X" on the dotted line
But wait, only in blood can you truly sign.
I see your hand shake, tell me the cause
Please no hesitation, take not a pause.

The action's complete so here's the deed
Tell me is the purchase what you need?
Won't you take note of the tiny fine print?
I see you read it with eyes that squint.

Never can you get a refund or an exchange
This policy is one the Devil and I did arrange
You bought everything in its current condition
Does such a disclaimer arouse any suspicion?

As now I'll take all you claim to hold dear
I paid the same only to be left with fear
I want it all — your mind, body and soul.
You hand it over giving away all your control.

Before you leave I'll give you your receipt
Signed by my hand, chock full of deceit
Do we both grasp that this ain't no lease
Truly I hope this transaction brings peace.

# Self-Serving Eulogy

On the roadside stands a forlorn forgotten cross
Warped wood strangled by weeds covered in moss
A memorial marking some unknown's tragic loss.

I step over gravel and stand on the dry ground
Birds nesting in the trees making the only sound
This hallowed place is where the lost are to be found.

There's no body buried beneath the dirt and grass
Nor is there any decomposition that comes to pass
Here, no funeral was held; no priest-man uttered mass.

The name burned onto the wood is the same as mine
Dates of birth and death are my haunting sign
I laid me to rest here amidst the towering pine.

Dead and wilted flowers litter the memorial's base
Here mourners gather before God to plead a case
For a time they are free of the demons they face.

A tear trickles down my cheek and falls to the dirt
That's just the beginning of the proof of my hurt
This emotion is like the Devil with whom I flirt.

With a sob stuck in my throat I turn away to leave
I'm just not willing nor able to stay here and grieve
That nightmare was only one the most evil can weave.

# Dutiful Remembrance

I have to remember where I came from
Especially when urges and cravings come
I can't forget the evil and hell
But on the glorious times I cannot dwell.

I remember the ride to jail so vividly
The day after I prayed to God timidly
Surrender allowed this plan to take shape
He came soaring in wearing a hero's cape.

I'm grateful now for everything I did
Thankful for a past that won't be hid
In the end I'll be a far better man
Falling in step with God's holy plan.

I can still hear the cell door slam
The door closed with the sharpest "BAM!"
Never before had I felt so alone
God used this time to make himself known.

I remember the overdose journey to death
And how she fought just to give me breath
Today I'm far beyond grateful to be alive
Such a glorious feeling to finally thrive

I am able to recall the needle's pain
On my arm I spread the crimson stain
I pray to God that I'll always remember
From frigid January to frosty December.

# Ghost Scars

Over the scar she ran her finger
A ghostly touch that yet will linger.
I was unsure of how I felt
Into my skin I saw marks melt.

A simple touch is so hard to crave
Demanding it be the one to save.
The memories came of a needle's prick
Wake up sober, try not to be sick.

The scars they speak in silence
Constant Recollection of the violence
This is the hell in me that I made
A holy temple that I so betrayed.

I trace the tissue so as not to weep
Then I lay myself down to sleep
Dreams replay and they never end
A lullaby for my brain to mend.

Where the arm bends the memories remain
A flash of yesterday that comes with pain
The scars spell out, "Helter Skelter"
Building a palace that is no shelter.

Did she grasp the depths of it all?
Or will she become a twelve step call
Scars help me practice what I preach
To a congregation I'd love to reach.

# Tailor Made Evil

I'm amazed at the evil I can do
My capacity for it seems to be great
It's not hard for me to hurt you
Who knew I could hold so much hate.

This fool strayed far from the light
I gave in to my darkest desires
It was so easy to fall to evil's might
So I wallowed in Hell's famed fires.

The darkness was all too consuming
It held me captive for a time so long
I lost hope in the light ever resuming
Reveling in despair was more than wrong.

Never did I mean to hurt anyone
My plans were okay if they only pained me
I forced many to live under my gun
They became hostages I wouldn't free.

I did things I grew up fearing
Came to be a trial to look into the mirror
What a joke thinking I was so endearing
Nothing could help me see any clearer.

I'm a better man than my past
Time will show how I was mistaken
Here's to hoping the present will last
Heretofore my future was always forsaken.

# Haunting Rangers

Through my past I watch ghosts come
Those unsettled spirits in search of home
Familiar transparent faces I can see through
Just long dead being's doing as they do.

I feel them creep through my weary mind
There I wonder what they're trying to find
Are they living out a haunting commission?
Not unlike soldiers on a fateful mission.

No leash or harness will hold them
Through my body's veins they still swim
I try to catch them in this phantom rodeo
But I'm the only spectator for this show.

What exactly do these ethereal friends seek?
I used to believe they fed only on the weak
But now I feel myself growing strong
Holding onto this false belief way too long.

Ghosts of my past they go from place to place
Painful death grimaces are etched on every face
Maybe with time we will all become friends
For now they remind me of my life's trends.

# Hold the Line

I'm sick and tired of this war
I've forgotten what I'm fighting for
Can someone tell me the end game?
Surely it is more than guilt or shame.

Long ago I fired my final shot
Yet the fight rages on heavy and hot
Where are the reserves I can deploy?
A commander's privilege has no joy.

I hold a long list of casualties
Each one pushed me past my abilities
The blood shed is not just mine alone
This crimson river made itself known.

It's come down to fists and bayonets
Now it is close quarters with my regrets
Overwhelmed the situation does demand
In the end only one of us will stand.

I've held this patch of hallowed ground
Still anticipating the bugle's last sound
After eternity I hear no clarion call
So here I wait for my final fall

In this battle there is never retreat
Until now all I've known is defeat
At last I see my sight becoming clear
Now, I believe my victory is near.

# I Have a Question

I have a question I must ask
Will your answer be equal to the task?
Where were you when the tables turned?
As flames consumed flesh that burned.

I have a question on my mind
Hoping to answer I won't decline
Why did you refuse to walk away?
As I lived in Hell every day.

I have a question in my heart
Your response may tear me apart
Why didn't you try and stop me
You seemed content to let me be.

I have a question waiting in line
If you don't answer, that's fine
Did you let me give up on dreams?
Thinking everything was as it seems.

I have a question to throw to you
Your response I know will be true
When did you know I wasn't alright?
Looking at me through crystal sight.

I have a question that yet remains
I'm ready for every answer that pains
Why did I readily become that man?
Another cog in God's favorite plan.

# Kill, Steal and Destroy

I've done my part to kill, steal and destroy
No past deed brought me any joy
I only delivered sorrow with grief
How it pains to be called a thief.

My words hurt and my actions stung
I need repentance like air in my lungs
Saying, "I'm sorry" doesn't mean a lot
Forgiveness is a battle trying to be fought.

I never meant to take and kill a soul
Never did I let God have his control
There is no going back what is now dead
No Lazarus effect for words unsaid.

Not every bruise and cut will fade
There's scars left of what I've made
From each one I've constructed a palace
Built on a broken foundation of malice.

Broken home? Try a tragically broken life
I destroyed her who I asked for my wife
Torn to pieces was the fabric of trust
All because the dope became a must.

I did my best to invade, pillage and burn
Now from those evil ways I must turn
In my wake lies scattered out rubble
Such is the result of my sad trouble.

# Open Title

Has heartbreak become a part of my life?
To my throat I hold my own knife
I'm the only hostage that I have left
The sole victim of the Devil's last theft.

In the shadows within lurks familiar pain
Who's to say feeling this drives me insane?
One by one the memories come as a flood
They are about as clear as pitch black mud.

The hurt comes up at all the wrong times
As if I need reminders for all of my crimes
It stops me on a heartbeat and a breath
What can I do to deliver this pain's death?

Tell me if this is what I signed up for
Who in their right mind fights this war?
Pain with Love, I guess is a risk we take
I hoped for joy yet I resented heartbreak.

I'll take it all at once or none at all
Unfortunately the pain is not heeding my call.
But no, the pain comes only as it really cares
I've asked God for help in countless prayers.

I wonder if I'll ever meet with Love again
Next time, will I be punished for every past sin?
There's fear left inside - fear of the unknown
How is it greater than the fear of being alone?

# Regrets Defined

Regrets are resentments towards the past
Sometimes they come on so very fast
Man or woman, we all come to know them
So we sing along with a broken hymn.

Of my regrets I can name a few
I'm guilty of having them, that's true
Anger came with many a lost chance
Like never asking that girl to dance.

Living in regret is no way to live
For another change anything you'd give
God doesn't deal in time machines
And memory replays all the scenes.

There's no going back through locked doors
Wishing for peace instead of life's wars
Choices dictate every heart's condition
The failure or success of your mission.

There's hope in that regrets can fade
Unless of course you'd rather they stayed.
In time internal wounds can heal
Leaving you surprised how you can feel.

Are we batting a thousand with regrets?
Striking out to feel like we are rejects
Where's regret when we seize the day?
That leaves one less devil to pay.

# Destination for Good Intentions

The road to Hell is paved with good intentions.
I know, as I helped to lay each cobblestone
No golden bricks exist there by any definition
The best laid route leads to the devil's throne.

Every single stone bears its own bloody footprint
The tracks lead onward but not away from.
A foreboding horizon is full of the dark's hint
Demons motion to the masses crying out, "Come!"

Towards black gates the road twists and turns
Lakes of fire beck the damned to enter in
Along the road reeks the flesh as it burns
The prince's henchmen tally up each dark sin.

Behind me intentions mythical road begins to fade
The pearled gates of Heaven are looming behind.
His fiery highness has already in full been paid
I slipped through his realm before I was dead.

I left behind so much on that painful road
In time my ghostly tracks will all but disappear
As to the roadside I cast off and away my load
The hate, misery, and regret piled high with fear.

Now I know where good intentions will always end
They drown in the pools filled with brimstones fire
Dying on the torture racks as they writhe and bend
Just another victim to my heart's inhuman desire.

# *Relationships*

# Fogging Memories

Memories cloud up as thick as smoke
They all seem like a sick, bad joke
Ghosts occupy every street and lane
Inside me they haunt me insane.

I see her face everywhere I go
That's just another amends to owe
Remembering good days and bad nights
I'm like a specimen underneath the lights.

Fate reminds me of everything I lost
As if I could have forgotten the cost
Why does Destiny play this game?
As if she needs any more fame.

What I recall is all so very tragic
It appears like a wizard's magic
Every memory is but a gravestone
Ghosts keep begging me to atone.

Phantoms of yesterday passing me by
Floating on another question of, "Why?"
They trap me, sinking in blackest bog
Overwhelmed, enveloped by time's fog.

God help me my memories have stayed
I hope, I pray every one will fade.
How many more will I have to face
Or are they with me on this race?

# Amb-i-ddiction

Boy, how I would love to hold her very close
Truly, I am starting to love her the utmost
The drugs are fast becoming a faded memory
It's all the same contained in my past's tragedy.
The taste of her kiss still lingers on my lips
To this day I can feel her on my fingertips
All I remember is that she tasted so sweet
Won't someone set this track onto repeat

I'm longing for the soft feel of her pale skin
There's no denying I yearn to touch her again
Would it matter if she became my new drug
My new fix would come from each tender hug.

I love how kissing her neck drives her so crazy
When I'm with her I'm so very far from lazy
Nothing even comes close to us being intimate
She's everything when I think of compassionate.
I so dig her body to me it's the read deal
Words can't describe exactly how good I feel
Hot damn I'm like a teenager all over again
If I stay with her I'm up for a sure win.

Ain't no joke that her bangin' body is hot
Oh Boy I'm craving her more than just a lot
In every way I guarantee you she is great
No doubt this separation is worth the wait.

# Call Me Crazy

Call me crazy but I think something's wrong
It's been five months, not terribly long.
Shouldn't I hurt more than just a little bit?
Don't think me a child throwing a fit.

Heartache should sting more like a blade
Yet here I sit questioning it as it fades
My stitched-up heart beats in my chest
Each convulsing beat seems less like a test.

Part of me wants to feel all that I fear
The other part refuses to shed even a tear.
Which part is right or wrong I can't decide?
Call me a coward but I haven't even tried.

To me writing her off just seems so terrible
But letting her presence remain is unbearable.
Karma and fate aren't giving their advice
Their punishing ways I'm unable to entice.

I fear I deserve worse than I'm getting
Phobia's the beast that keeps me regretting
So my guard is up against a blackened sky
The coming storm is one I know won't lie.

Shouldn't I be thankful my heart's intact?
Yet still I try to take pieces and subtract.
Now pain plus time does not equal sorrow
Call me crazy but its pain I trying to borrow.

# One Hit Wonder

I can still see her hit the pipe
Thinking proudly, "She's my type!"
The glass burned my fingertips
As she inhaled two giant rips.

I dropped the piece to the floor
Every hoping she would want more
Smarting from skin that scorched
I knew our souls I had torched.

I can still see the smoke she exhaled
Billowing premonitions I had failed.
Acidic clouds that stung my eyes
All to a chorus of demonic cries.

I picked up the pipe in my hand
Knowing well the journey I planned.
Recoiling from the chemical's bite
I knew our souls would lose the fight.

I can still see her eyes go wide
Her soul escaped just as it died.
Pale skin instantly flushed red
With it the future was left for dead.

I took my turn for the next hit
Hoping only to find I'd get lit
Grimacing as I choked on the fumes
I knew my actions forecasted doom.

# Ghosts

I'm okay living with these ghosts
They sure make memorable hosts.
Forever will I be knowing them
Their hauntings have been grim.

I can't run away or so it seems
These phantoms appear in all my dreams
I'm being reminded of my past
These hauntings always tend to last.

Ethereal beings begin to linger.
Have I forgotten about life's ringer?
These hauntings will always remain
'Cuz I fight on a different plane.

Not every ghost can be excised
They are fed by how I lied
I accept this is how it is now
It helps that I know the how.

We all have our own kind haunting
Yet the past remains always taunting
It's like living in a haunted house
Thriving as the trap house's mouse.

No, I didn't want to see them again
I hardly care if they can grin
Yet, they live in my cold memory
Just an uncounted casualty.

# Hanging

She left me hanging by a thread
"I hope you die" That's what I said
For a year we pushed the envelope
Countless nooses tied in a rope.

The hangman laughed like a child
In my struggle for air I went wild
Never did I utter a final word
If I had, no one would have heard.

Course threads cut into my skin
These gallows erected by my sin.
No one moves to help cut me down
Constricted, I can't make a sound.

My lungs feel like they will burst
This demise goes beyond the worst
Feet kick air seeking out a ledge
My former life pushed to the edge.

This destiny comes with not a surprise
Ramifications for all my splendid lies
Please say I met Fate as a man
From my punishment I never ran.

I left me here hanging by a sliver
Death's cold hands caused a shiver
Blackness takes hold of my vision
Guess this means I won my mission.

# Remember the Night

Remember the night we rented a room
So far gone in a drug addict's gloom
I can't recall that night in detail
Something tells me we hid from Hell.

Remember the night we stayed up 'til dawn
You were my queen and I your pawn
If memory serves we shot a lot of dope
Hanging by a thread onto the Devil's rope

Remember the night we sang but did not dance
A lullaby that defined our sick romance
My memory can't replay that sinister hymn
Still we waltzed on a breaking tree limb

Remember the night my hand struck you down
The impact echoed in waves across the town
A recollection exists of your skin being bruised
Such a shame that you were so easily abused.

Remember the night that I threatened to leave
On your knees you begged grabbing my sleeve
All too easily I remember how I stayed
In hindsight I can see we were betrayed.

Remember the night we mocked the feral sun
Like fools we were convinced it was all fun
Don't let me remember just so I can forget
The evening star rules until the fabled sunset.

# Heartbreak Defined

Pray tell what is a broken heart?
Is it the end or is it a start?
A chapter closes so one can begin
This pain is known by all men.

I've had my share as have you
"This too shall pass" is so very true
Sometimes that's hard to believe
When all you know is how to grieve.

Yes, parting is such sweet sorrow
When time is something we borrow
The words we fear are, "Good-bye"
Causing even the coldest of us to cry.

Who of us knows not of heartache?
We sail alone across pain's lake
Though we wish we were a stranger
Unknown, untouched by love's danger.

My heart is stitched over with scars
Because I was shooting for the stars
Such is the price that we all pay
Just for knowing Love for the day.

So, count up all the loves lost
Tally them up to add to the cost
Heed the fact that there is more
I guarantee Love's keeping score.

# My Number 1 Fan – Mom
## 5/14/2017 – Mother's Day

Its thirty years now that we've been together
No way could I have asked for a better mother
You've been so strong throughout all these years
In times both good and bad in smiles and tears.

Seldom have I shown you my truest appreciation
Shame on me, for you gave me my creation
It's never too late to start saying, "I love you"
Giving you all that I owe is the least I can do.

I've done things to you that broke heart and soul
It must've hurt like Hell to see me out of control
You taught me better than to steal or to lie
At some point you watched a sweet little boy die.

The man I became was but a shadow of that boy
Times far and few did I cause you any joy
I'm responsible for countless numbers of gray hairs
The same amount you plead, sent up in many prayers.

I'll never forget how you stood by me all the time
Even when my actions had nothing in reason or rhyme
No matter what I did, I never pushed you away
That's unconditional love from what all the people say.

The time has come for me to make one final amends
I will live out my life for forgiveness of my sins
Any battle I can handle cuz of what you taught
This is my chance for absolution so I'll give it a shot.

"I love you, Mom," you can take that to the bank
As far as heroes go at the top spot you hold rank
I'm far beyond blessed to call you my Mom,
You're the best there is, hell, you're the bomb.

# Perfect Poison

The perfect poison is all we were.
In every way, I was toxic for her.
We both drank death by the vial
Every side effect caused us a new trial.

I can't fathom what I was thinking
The toxins kept my poor heart sinking.
Like Romeo I was so quick to swallow
Yet death was never quick to follow.

The dark brown liquid tasted so bitter
Made me feel like I threw a no-hitter.
It hit my stomach and gave me a high
For a moment I swore I could fly.

Together we lay on a gilded funeral pyre
Our situation dissolved into one so dire.
Everything we drank was a sour brew
Chased down with words, "I love you."

Our poison was of the utmost refreshment
Causing us to die of our thirsty resentment.
Now I'm choking on stale dusty breath
I'm familiar now with the taste of death.

This toxin is stuck down deep in my throat
It is as deep as Camelot's mythical moat.
I reckon I can say I'm not really dying
Tears shed are the poison I am crying.

# Pray, Hope and Believe

I PRAY that she is happy in the end
That's the hope I am trying to send
All while fixing fences needing a mend.

She is in my prayers day and night
I ask God to make her future bright
This selfless request will make me alright.

The joy we shared was the wrong kind
Problems were all we could ever find
We must have driven Cupid out of his mind.

I HOPE she will learn a happy song
That sounds better than singing it wrong
For melodic joy she's waited for so long.

Will I hear her voice again? Probably not.
That's fine, at least we gave us a shot
The opportunity begins to mean a lot.

It's crazy that I accept she's moved on.
Still, it hurts to know that she's gone
Yet no one can be forced to be my pawn.

I BELIEVE I'm next after she gets her turn.
My past is the teacher from whom I learn
Before this it was my Hell that made me burn.

# When an Angel Cries

I bore witness to an angel crying today
Her tears failed to damper out Hell's fire
Words of comfort were not even mine to say
To rid her of distress was my one desire.

Salty streaks graced a long ago radiant face
I could all but taste the tears that fell
She looked lost, cut off from God's grace
Was she waiting to hear Heaven's brass bell?

None and nothing could catch her sweet tears
The sky's softest cloud couldn't absorb them
Did she weep for me, my shame, and my fears?
As she mourned I cried out my final hymn

The pretty countenance before me turned red
Riddled with pain I sent my heart out to her
Her suffering like a cancer in me spread.
Then the world I knew began to turn blue.

What earthly tragedy can ever cause an angel to cry?
Only a fool puts his burdens on her soft shoulders
It's such a shame she must bear my every lie
I'm the only one to blame for her growing colder.

Like every other human male I did turn my back
I was overwhelmed by the situation's single demand
Leaving her alone to fend off my sorrow's attack
Another angel forsaken and left behind as planned.

# Pards (to Jeff)

You say you weren't there for me
Yet a different truth is what I see
Life went on while I stood still
Chasing the high from a magic pill.

How can I fault you for your life?
A Navy man with kids and a wife.
Over the years you sure made me proud
Your selfless friendship always rings loud.

Never did you judge or beat me down
You tried making a smile of my frown
How you held me when I would stumble
Like China's Wall you wouldn't crumble.

I owe you a debt I am unable to pay
Let me try by living sober every day
Only God above knows what is due
How grateful I am He gave me you.

We've shared laughs and times so grand
Better than the best laid plan
The memories we have we can't measure
Each one is a gift of the truest treasure.

Eighteen years you've been at my side
In you I still rightfully confide
What comes next will be the best
Our brotherhood can take any test.

# Pops

It's almost funny we find ourselves here again
Like a Shakespearean tragedy wrapped in a grin
Truthfully, Dad, this isn't what I had planned.
I saw myself following your every demand.

Somewhere along the way I went left before right
Guess that explains why I made everything a fight.
I still find it hard to believe everything I did.
My actions were the same as an immature kid.

"Build others up," that's one thing of many that you said.
For a while I tried to follow everywhere you led
When I let life get the upper hand I was wrong
Never did I think I'd suffer for a time so long.

After a while I found it easier to make poor choices
I even got good at blocking out the smart voices
My pride grew as I stayed the same little boy
Arrogance is like a gun in that it's not a toy.

I can't go back in time and fix the past from here
It's in my power to create a future I hold dear
You've given me so much and that's hard to repay
Now watch me succeed in life and make my own way.

It's true that not a one of us is close to perfect
Though you had many chances, you never made me a reject.
It's no wonder at all that you're my true hero
You never made me feel little or less than zero.

I'm grateful more than ever for the chances we get
The memories we share are far too strong to forget.
You've taught me a lot more than I'll ever truly know.
After thirty years it seems I'm ready to grow.

# Three Words

I've said a whole lot and not all of it was true.
How much was a lie when I'd say, "I love you."
I figured my words would make others' hearts glow
Now in hindsight I see my words were merely a show.

My actions didn't back up the things that I said
I always figured my little play knocked 'em all dead
How wrong to think that my words didn't deceive
It's sickening to see what I used to believe.

"I love you" is something special we all say.
Leave it to me to make them ring in a hollow way
Too busy loving myself made it impossible to share
Yet, I was so quick to pledge how much I care.

Sanctity fled my lips every time that I spoke
Everyone took my words as a bittersweet joke
I spoke as if I was a blasphemous hypocrite
How could anyone believe when my word was shit?

The three words, "I love you" speaks in volumes
We give them power that takes us and consumes
How can simple words wield over us so much power?
They either yield a taste so sweet or so sour.

One day I hope I can live by the words I speak
Such an honorable goal is among many I seek
Honor is no longer a foregone demise for my word
I'm joining and running with an honest living herd.

# She Said

"You lied," she said, "so, so many times"
A reminder of all of my crimes
Red rimmed eyes did not meet her gaze
I refused to confess any of my ways.

"Watch," she said "as we finally end"
Nothing left on which I can depend
Why God, oh why, did she remain?
Both of us gluttons for the pain.

"God knows," she said, "Things are amiss."
Forlorn silence begging for her kiss.
Suspicious minds came with the deal
Her paranoia this thief couldn't steal.

"I don't," she said "think I understand."
There we were at Custer's last stand
Insanity's actions went along unread
She could only mourn what was unsaid.

"Your faith," she said, "is far from strong"
I knew her words couldn't be wrong
So of God or Satan I did implore
Fearful of everything lying in store.

"Good bye," she said, "and even good luck"
Said I, "Au revoir, I give not a fuck."
So she was gone with that final blow
Then I knew I'd hit a new low.

# Call Before You Fall

I made a call hoping to make a choice
A part of me hoped to hear her voice
Another part wanted to get so much more
Now I wonder what I called her for.

Silence enveloped us for most of the call.
Initial proof nothing has changed at all.
The conversation was so inadequately inept
It seemed our words were heavy with debt.

Those few minutes seemed to last forever
I couldn't wait for the connection to sever
Awkward silence managed to take a hold
I realized nothing changed from days of old.

With the call's termination I let out a sign
Found myself asking the mirror exactly why.
I knew then that affection had moved on
And so I accepted that she too is gone.

I should have known it wouldn't end well
Some relationships are just doomed to fail
Still, I don't regret picking up the phone
It is not like that makes me any more alone.

At least now she won't become another "What if"
There's no use crying over a casualty that's stiff
I now mark her name off my ink scourged list
God makes me grateful for the times we kissed.

# When Pigs Fly

I have not luck at all with girls
May as well be hunting rare pearls
The game of Love used to be a joke
I'm left in the dust trying not to choke.

"I like you" seems so childish to say
In my warped mind it's the only way
When will I outgrow this boy so shy?
Guess I'll wait to see if pigs can fly.

I've chased women as if this was a game
Mostly the pursuit resulted in more shame
Now I remember, "Be careful what you wish for"
It's guaranteed that Cupid is keeping score.

My luck is shot and it must be my fault
Every time it was I that forced Love to halt
Like a gambler gone bust I'll lay a bet
When the house calls is when I will fret

If I have no luck then what's left
Of hope and faith I've become bereft
Yet again Love and Life deals me a hand
Let it be now that I draw a line in the sand.

# Words So Brave

I'm waiting to take a leap of infantile new faith
But scared as if I saw someone's haunting wraith.
Truly, courage will be required to say what I must
That's how I know this is love more than its lust.

Hard to believe that I let it come down to this
I was wrong to walk away from her sweet kiss
But in a backwards way I kind of spared her life
I took someone else hostage on the edge of a knife.

Today I'm grateful I had nerve enough to walk away
I kept her from experiencing the price I would pay
My love for her has laid dormant but remained strong
Yes, it is a shame that this has taken far too long

Of all I could say, my words are reduced to three
I hope and pray that to this day she still loves me.
Words are nowhere near as strong as a man's actions
My best laid plans failed for a lack of any traction.

What I want to get and to give I had better earn
No longer am I damned for my past's forsaken turn
Forgiveness came that I never really had expected.
I figured we were a past we never really perfected.

Breaking these words leaves me feeling as cold as a grave
Oh my girl, without the drugs am I really that brave
I want to show you what love means from a man
Please be a part of my newly written down plan.

I don't have much left of which I can speak
My knees are knocking and I'm feeling so weak.
This takes bravery if you'll allow me to be frank.

Here it goes: "I love you" and it still rings true
With another chance I know I'll see us through.
Saying that has taken a weight off of my chest.
Now all I can do is sit and hope for the best.

I guess what happens next is up to you
Honestly losing another person's love is a big fear
Maybe by God's grace we'll do this one more time,
If nothing else I hope that you enjoyed the rhyme.

# Dying Love

How long does it take love to fade?
I can't count the heartache paid
There are times I can help reminisce
The taste comes back of every kiss.

They say wounds heal over time
I can't find a reason or a rhyme
Madness of love is all consuming
Waiting for life to start resuming.

The first time it took many years
Having to come to grip with my fears
I had chased love but all in vain.
She laughed at me with disdain.

Love will come and so she will go
She drags her victims along in tow
This desire remains a foul temptress
I play her game only to regress.

No the memories are more spaced out
And a resolution I far from in doubt
Every day and it is getting better
In time I won't be Love's debtor

Love will grow from all that died
Its patience I have seldom tried
No, the good is not yet undone
It reappears with the rising sun.

# A Hand to Hold

In a crowded room I feel alone
Like a kid from a broken home
I do miss holding someone close
Now my arms reach for a ghost.

I'm surrounded by couples in love
That's all I'm left thinking of
So I clasp my hands in prayer
With God I play Truth or Dare.

I sweat at the scent of perfume
Damning this loneliness' sweet doom
Craving the bitter most of kisses
Launching dreams and forlorn wishes.

Laughter assaults my burning ears
As my eyes hold back salty tears
The sounds of love seem to prevail
Making me and how I can foil.

Where's the joy in being single?
Missing how love makes me tingle
Is love something that I forget?
Doing such has caused me regret.

No one likes to feel this way
Living to hear what Love will say
When all I want is a hand to hold
This is enough to make me feel old.

# Fallen Angel

There goes another fallen angel
By my grip she would strangle
I walked her right to the ledge
With a lie she went over the edge

With broken wings it's hard to fly
I clipped her feathers with every lie
Like a baby bird she fell from the nest
Her wings too fragile for the test.

Will she be a notch in my belt?
A victim to the hand I dealt
The casualty list adds another name
How many dead just to play my game.

With God she surely conversed
Even while His name I cursed
Her halo I broke into horns
So like me she would be torn.

I watched her plummet to earth
To another demon I gave birth
Her wings burned against the sun
As I was her antiaircraft gun.

The world watched an angel fall
Arms reached out in a distress call
I pushed them down to turn away
Devoid of hope that we will stay.

# *Recovery*

# Lust to Love

Everything I wanted was right in front of me
Yet I kept myself blind, unwilling to see
Playing the victim only got me so far
It's like wishing on a faraway star.

What did I gain from selling my soul?
Looking for anything to make me whole
I let the chemicals flow through my veins
Whatever it took to kill off all my pains.

I shot up lust chasing love's lost high
Overdosing while I screamed at the sky
While in pursuit my heart turned cold
Selling off everything I'd already sold.

Here I am starting over back at square one
After so many times this has lost its fun
I'm not so alone like I thought before
That's courage enough to walk through the door

Love, true love, she is right by my side
Running from her is all I ever tried
She's reaching out with a thousand hands
I want her in all my future plans

Drugs and lust they only do so very much
Either way they kept me out of touch
So now with this love I hope I'll stay
I've met failure in every other way.

# Fight for Life

I have lived my life as if it was a war
Fighting battle after battle and nothing more
In so many instances I've lived in vain
There is little wonder why I know pain.

My life I mapped out to end in my glory
Thirty years into life and have I got a story.
The number of my age seems to be really a lie
Made older by the tears I refuse to cry.

Am I like a soldier who is trying to atone?
Needing praise while craving to be left alone?
I've dodged Death and I've left him behind
Still Fate demands I pay her with my mind.

There's no graveyard that my life has made
No headstones in rows that are neatly laid
Is there an end to living hoping for a fight?
I feel this is a type of punishing blight.

What is left to face in the approaching years?
How many battles resulting in unknown tears
Only time will tell of all of yesterday's tomorrows
While today's yesterday drowns in its sorrow.

I have been wrong to live in such a bad way
Never seeing how blessed I am to live today
The wars I made never even got to exist
Over time I thought it was alright to resist.

# Ashes and Dust

Now I feel like I can lay my past to rest
In a grave six feet deep I'll lay a casket
Inside are memories of the worse and the best
They're buried together in that funeral basket.

"Rest in Peace" the tombstone silently declares
A final eulogy echoes over the filled in grave
Whispers rise up to Heaven on wings of prayers
As the minister reads from Holy words that save.

Dirt thumps down on the top of the wooden lid
Like rain pouring down from a leaden sky
The shovels dump dirt on my past's final bid
Beneath the earth I'll let all my memories lie.

Flowers are left by the black-garbed mourners
Bright colors a splash against all the gray stone
A glimpse of smiles in all the cemetery's corners
Mementos of love cause the graves to seem alone.

In farewell I say "Ashes to ashes, dust to dust"
So I turn away and walk back to the hearse
Leaving the bodies of time to erode into rust
With every step taken I'm free at last of my curse.

Raise a glass with me and say a fond farewell
Life goes on without me holding onto the past
Regretting what can't change is the path to Hell
Bury your regrets and life will change very fast.

# No Rain, No Gain

Outside the window I watch it rain
Days like this numb me from pain
I sit back and smile as the sky cries
The angels are mourning all that dies.

Am I out of place wearing this smile?
Truly I hope it keeps raining a while
Other folks tend to look so very sad
For me gray skies cause me to be glad.

Don't get me wrong I like sunny days too
Rain or shine I'm happy all the way through
There's something to love in stormy days
I'm like a criminal finally free of his ways.

There's joy to be found even in a storm
Even for those for whom joy ain't the norm
I used to have a black cloud over my head
Those times I didn't want to get out of bed.

Sometimes the lightening comes across scary
Really it's quite beautiful on the contrary
I used to look at life in ways I was wrong
Now life's storms got me singing a new song.

# Year Down

Oh, it's amazing what changes in a year
Things fade away that once were so dear
The first thing to become new is the clock
Every day and month is under key and lock

Tomorrow is impossible for anyone to predict
Time's inevitable passing is God's harsh verdict
No crystal ball awaits us to divulge its tales
Every hour's death is marked by chiming bells.

Everything I had then has gone and died
Yesteryear's bones in a barren crypt reside
Now in hindsight I can see all the clues
Had I listened I wouldn't have met the blues

Looking back I see how I wasn't close to right
There is a lot to be said for having hindsight
Nowadays everything tends to make sense
Yet the future still keeps me in suspense.

I'm working very hard to make a new start
The old life is almost too much for my heart
I refuse to keep doing this over and over again
Today I pay for yesterday's rampant sin.

Never could I have guessed about today
Last year was like a Texas storm in May
Where I'm at now is behind a waiting dawn
In the breadth of one year only evil is gone.

# Rearview Mirror – My View

It's been a while since I've travelled those roads
A year later I'm not stumbling under the heavy loads
Crossroads I crossed day by the day aren't the same
Hell, I can't even remember either street's name.

I saw my ghost as it travelled down that route
Deep in my throat I had to suppress a shout
The phantom and I at one point we locked eyes
How surprised was I to watch my past at it dies.

As I drove away I didn't look over my shoulder
I gladly left behind a body to begin to molder
Regrets were left behind trying to thumb a ride
Such relief is palpable without guilt by my side.

The wind now blows across the streets I left behind
See the phantoms I created in my sick mind
Tumbleweeds skip across the striped asphalt lanes
Only dusty whispers from sewn-shut lips yet remains.

Over and along barren boulevards my memory travels
In my mind's wake my threadbare past unravels
The ghosts fade away with the peace of acceptance
Letting old roads pass by is my way of repentance.

My view in the rearview mirror is clouded by dust
What lies behind the veil is something to take on trust
The road ahead is imperfect but it's an improvement
Travelling this route is one that demands commitment.

# To the Reader

Don't feel bad for me and my addiction
Understand it became a part of my convictions
I chose to live life as a strung out addict
A pro at living with the pain I did inflict.

Don't feel sorry for me over my disease
Understand it's okay so your mind will be at ease
I have set my sights on some solid recovery
Now I'm looking forward to new discovery.

Don't blame my actions on this illness
Let me 'fess up to earn my forgiveness
I'm not perfect when I'm sober or when high
My past proves that truth to be far from a lie.

Don't think that I haven't seen some hell
There was many a time when all was not well.
I know now I convinced myself I was okay
Deception birthed from all the lies I'd say.

Don't hold it against me for not doing this sooner
Open your eyes to behold I was a loser.
I won't regret a past I am unable to change
Let's look to the future as it comes into range.

# Past Be Gone

The past has died and so I have moved on
Yesterday has perished with today's new dawn
I used to be a long shackle bound slave
Barely living with one foot in an early grave.

Again my life has been granted a new lease
That must be the explanation for this peace
For too long I've been doing this all alone
Leaving calls for help on a broken old phone.

Now I believe I'm travelling on the best path
I no longer expect the hell of God's wrath
My feet move forward in the slowest motion
As my mind begins to comprehend sobriety's notions.

I'm really not afraid of what is waiting ahead
Drawing breath sure beats lying there dead.
What awaits me is a taste of all my ability
For most of my life I've focused on my frailty.

I have hope now where none existed before
My eyes see a newly opening chapter's door
There's no hesitation as I eagerly walk through
This I do for me for my future and you.

Hopefully those I love most will stay by my side
Something tells me it's gonna be a real fun ride
I can forgive myself now and God knows I've tried
So, I've moved on and I've let the past finally die.

# Price Tag

The final price tag of my past has become clear
Balance due was what I misconceived as dear
Now what I see is that I didn't pay very much
The method of payment is a type I can't touch.

It wasn't my heart nor my soul that the Devil took
Even though it was my very foundation he really shook
The evil one took from me what was so dark and bad
For many years I had given him everything I had.

My fears and deprivations stayed on the killing floor
Without my self-inflicted horrors I felt I was poor
What's emerging is an unknown entity lost to time
A human form approaches in a body that's prime

I paid with the parts of me I've labelled the worst
That half of me was what I always had put first
What I let go of I don't care to ever see again
All that I lost is what is envied by all men.

All along I've been looking at this in the wrong way
What was charged to me seemed a lot for me to pay
Through the years I figured this was a battle lost
Now I'm glad I've paid up and shouldered the cost.

Unfortunately I wasn't the only one who took the fall
I always guessed I would have to give up it all
The casualties I'm sorry to say could be spared
Don't think I don't know that each of them cared.

# Wounds + Healing = Scars

Wounds heal, scars grow
Becoming prizes we like to show.
On the outside, that's how it tends to go.

Hearts break, stitches appear
Healing us all of the pain we fear.
On the inside, that's how closure draws near.

Eyes fill up, tears fall
The rain splatters on our walls
This emotional deluge is undertaken by all.

Hands tremble, fingers quake
Busily trying to repair every mistake
Our body's tools never given a fair shake.

Teeth grind, lips seal
Unspoken words are unable to heal
Imprisoned tongues can't say how we feel.

Stomach churns, heart pounds,
Pumping blood so fast like racing hounds
Flooding the ears with noise unlike many sounds.

Knees knock, legs will fold
To the ground you will fall so cold
Pillars of strength no longer able to uphold.

Jay Koch

Wounds heal, scars fade
Becoming receipts of what we've paid
On the inside, it's how each of us is made.

# Rock Bottom

I hit rock bottom and laughed in its face
Pity that I never learned my true place
I look up from the bottom of this pit
My legs are mired in a swamp of shit.

People pass by and look down on me
No one bothers to help set me free
I don't blame them for not trying
Turning deaf ears to all of my crying.

No ladder exists for me to climb the wall
Nor is there a potion to make me tall
Am I stuck here forever and a day
I want out but don't know the way.

The needle and more put me down here
Pushed from the edge by every fear
Nothing padded my landing at the end
Now its SOS signals I am trying to send.

"Wait!" a voice calls from the far off light.
There! A head and shoulders come into sight
"I've been where you are," so says the voice
And, "I'm an addict and not by my choice!"

A ladder comes down constructed of rope
In my soul I feel the glimmer of hope
"Climb up a step at a time," comes the cry
My feet and hands are willing to try.

# Streets

I've traveled streets so poorly paved
Asphalt and concrete both depraved
All our angels have been enslaved
While deep inside my heart is staved.

Phantoms fly above man's lost highway
With our angels and our demons at play
Standing among the mourners we pray.

Remember how everything went wrong
Same verse but in a different song
The chorus changes as we all go along.

Hell's road is paved by a good intention
To the Devil's toll all give attention
Yet the price to play is not to mention.

A journey made right went to Hell
I got lost somewhere on the trail
What's left to measure on Guilt's scale?

The destination searched for is unfound
Amazing Grace, my dear, cannot be bound
A chorus in harmony will not dent sound.

I crawled down streets lost to sight
Crawling through a tunnel towards the light
Around me is blackness as cold as night
Yet you claim this journey is worth the fight.

# Start Over

I thought that old life would be forever
But I went awry thinking myself so clever
Slowing down was never even a thought
Chasing the dragon for one more shot.

No, I'm not surprised I ended up lost
Until now I refused to fathom any cost
Truthfully, how I lived wasn't done for free
Running from the devil as he pursued me.

There's no excuse that hasn't been said
Hard to speak from the lips of the dead
Words can only rebuild a few bridges burned
They didn't stop the tables as they turned.

Now I get to learn to start over again
No matter what I'll have to face my sin.
Darkness showed me that I'm a good man
It showed me the true Glory of God's plan.

This isn't the first time but maybe the last
My first thirty years went by way too fast
What comes next is going to be a wild ride
I avoided it all the times I had lied.

Why was I content living, hoping to just die?
Hoping, praying that time wouldn't ever fly
I compromised to a poor way of living
Secretly full of a new kind of misgiving.

# Nothingness

Is there nothing left I can say or write?
No reasons justify the pain of the fight
Words of substance can only travel so far
Trivial meanings that burn up like a star

Nothing is sufficient enough to describe the pain
I am left staring at old labels full of disdain
Maybe firsthand alone will they know my hurt
The kind that buries one alive under tons of dirt.

Does nothing explain the bitter darkness I miss?
Am I like Romeo craving Juliette's final kiss?
Deep down inside this absence has made a void
The better angels of my nature work 'til it's destroyed

Nothing depicts the foreign limbo I am in
Stuck between then and now until I start again
Never before have I known such shades of grey
What liar swore relief by living only for today?

When will nothing fade into this yesterday's affair?
Eternally it lurks within as an unspoken prayer
If this is all I'll ever have then what's to lose?
Please understand this isn't the damnation I choose.

Nothing remains waiting to divulge a final serenade
An endless melody with a chorus to never fade
The only gamble left to lose is mine to embrace
Will this Nothingness be the last I'll face?

# God's Glorious Gift

What is this glory that I behold?
I'm wrapped up in the angel's fold
Am I on the outside looking in?
My reflection looks back with a grin.


I see God's mercy and delight
The things against which I used to fight
Acceptance and love I have chased
But it was only my own wrath I faced.


I am a son in whom he is well pleased.
It's up to me if the day is seized
His mission for me I see so plain
It's one borne of all of my pain.


His forgiveness always by my side
The very thing that has never lied.
Through all the hell He never gave up
Even when I drank from Evil's cup.


In the small things I see his splendor
This mighty God who is my defender
From Him I cannot turn and run
He brings good from what was undone.


God's plan it supersedes my own
His benevolent side is one always shown
I feel His embrace holding me close
A perfect love that I needed the most.

# Amazing Grace

Can I turn this life around?
How are the long lost found?

Don't think I am too far gone
I have breath left to see the dawn
When did I say this is enough?
No doubt life surely got rough.

This is my high water mark
See me emerge from the dark.
The worst long ago it passed.
Sure enough it could not last.

What kind of life can I build?
Now God is my sturdy shield
From ash the Phoenix will rise
Saved from an untimely demise.

Looking forward the future is unclear
There will be pain next to fear
The past it still lingers about
Living for today is beyond doubt.

I find myself much less afraid
There's acceptance for what I've paid
See me back at the starting line
Some would say that is a sign

Has this life really turned around?
By Amazing Grace I've been found.

# 11 Months, 3 Weeks and 3 Days
# (Now)

I've been clean for almost a year
Yes, I like what's going on in here.
I read my past like it's a book
Every page I gave a good hard look.

I've wanted this more than I can remember
Until now I refused to flirt with surrender
Everything I wanted I readily gave away
Everything I need came back day by day.

Being locked up is not how I planned it.
For some this is the path that we get
That's what it took to set me free
I paid willingly so sober I can be.

I look back on all that transpired
Seeing the evil of which I desired
I know the hell that I can bring
So focus on the good of which I sing.

So much destruction is left in my wake
There's so much it can be hard to take
And what lies ahead is anyone's guess
I accept in life there will be stress.

Eleven months are what I can claim
This time around I seek not fame
What I need is a year plus more
That's a goal worth fighting for.

# Twelve Years

The last twelve years were a test
Yet I see I never tried my best
I surrendered in all the wrong ways
Trying just to survive the days.

Time passed so slowly yet so fast
The days and months seemed to last
In the sky the sun stood still
As I drank and drugged my fill

What was I trying to hide from?
Afraid of whatever was meant to come
Both failure and success haunted me
Enslaved to life and never set free.

Over the years I ran in slow motion
Poorly spending my pent up devotion
Holding tight to a most tragic song
Reinventing a way of living so wrong.

My peers left me in the dust
Turning away as I burned with lust.
In the end there's no one to blame
At the end, nothing was the same.

To the last twelve years I won't go back
I'm learning to live with all I lack
So now I will take another exam
This time around I give a damn.

# Have You Or Can You

Have you ever heard the angels sing?
Or taken time to hear the bells ring?
Can you find joy here on Earth?
Or step back just to see your worth?

Have you ever truly smelled the flowers?
Or marveled over all of God's powers?
Can you live every day to the fullest?
Or walk away from being the coolest?

Have you ever tried counting your blessings?
Or forsaken everything that is stressing?
Can you take pride in what was done?
Or sit back to enjoy the rising sun?

Have you found love in what is holy?
Or spent time living life so slowly?
Can you stay honest through the day?
Or face devils who demand their pay?

Have you lived the cry of, "Carry on?"
Or played your queen before a pawn?
Can you make it past the adverse?
Or give thanks over a holy verse.

Have you seen God in your humility?
Or recognized your own true ability?
Can you offer a broken man's prayer?
Or love someone you know who cares.

# Twelfth Step Call

"I want to get sober," he said
Is he tired of the demons he fed?
"Well, let's give it a try," I replied
Further proof God has never died.

Whatever help I can give I will
God knows I've seen addiction kill
I can't dictate just how this will go
Truly, I hope he has hit his low.

I must share what was shared with me
The duty of helping others I finally see
This love I have is for giving away
Those are the dues I am able to pray.

I don't hold this duty to be cheap
It goes further than just skin deep
For God's help I am quick to ask
Without Him I am unequal to any task.

I've prayed, "God, let me help someone.
Let me show sobriety is indeed fun."
He answered me and gave me a charge
Through Him no battle is far too large.

My friend's ultimate choice is his alone
I am an instrument of my God's throne
Should I save a life the debt is paid
To offer my hand I am not afraid.

# One Step or One Mile

I used to be too scared to walk through this door
Like a green soldier as he's shipped off to war
Going from one life style to the next is so daunting
Especially as your closet's ghosts keep haunting

Oh, the years it has taken to cross this old threshold
One too many faces I've watched go and grow old
A solitary yard became my life's longest yard
'Twas I that made doing what's right so hard

The doors been open wide since I was eighteen
I lived hard thinking Life owed me every thing
I mocked the white robed doorman as he waited
Down in my soul I made him one of the hated.

A forlorn, haunting wind blew through the doorway
This poor fool didn't hear the balance I'd pay
The wind was God's voice begging me to step through
Such a sweet symphony ending in his, "I love you."

To me the opening became barred by curtains of pain
I looked in like a sailor through sheets of heavy rain
The blind may not see but they can at least hear
Yet I shut my eyes and ears to every little fear.

Thirty years old, as a man the doorway I now breach
Grabbing onto warm hands long held out trying to reach
I step through knowing yet more doors I will face
No worries exist about finishing strong in life's rac

# Faith & Redemption

# Before and After

What was I way back when?
Barely a coward among men
A grinning fool fueled by lies
Repeating inanity in all my tries.

I can't explain by any excuse
So point back to every abuse.
Action outweighed a paltry word
Every promise made was made absurd.

Don't think that I'm unaware
There's ramifications for every prayer
Did I really want what I asked?
It was pain refusing to be masked.

Can you see what I'm becoming?
A man ready to quit running
I face trials and I face fire
I'm born of a well-honed liar.

Yesterday has become exactly that
No longer the Devil's welcome mat
To the Heavens I'll tilt my face
Sufficient for me is God's grace.

Please don't feel sorry for me
This is everything I hoped to be
A man broken and made willing
Accepting memories that are chilling.

# Dawn

The dawn has arrived at long last
New light begins to consume the black
Yesterday has died along with the past
My old ways I will never get back


A new day has sprouted from the dirt
I've nurtured the present with love
These roots are buried in my heart
But my branches reach for God above.


This smile adorns my weathered face
The new day's light shines over you.
I've cross the finish line for the race
My trophy and triumph both ring true.


There's a hope that's rising with the sun
Can you hear it flutter on Angel's wings?
On this day I know the good is done
Harken to hear my future as it sings.


Today is enough to cause me to smile
When is the last time I craved the light?
Happiness has been absent to a while
I'm glad yesterday has fled my sight.


From here so much is about to begin
Hope permeates from any and everywhere
I'm not shackled any longer to my sin
This happened on the life of a prayer.

# Flickering Flame

Beyond the fence I see the same old flame
It's so familiar to me I should give it a name.
Over the months it's become a beacon so bright
Constantly it burns far away both day and night.

I can't explain how but this gives me hope
I'm like a condemned man told he'll escape the rope
When I see the flame burning my heart does glow
To me this flickering talisman seems more than show.

I never saw this flame when I was out and free
Distractions in life's facets helped me not to see
Can't help wondering if it will be there when I'm out
But for now the flame's existence I don't doubt.

The cause of this sign is of little or no concern
All I know is I seek it out hoping it continues to burn
It's like the burning bush that old Moses saw
I'm not afraid nor tempted to still withdraw.

When I step outside it's to the south that I gaze
Like a man with a thousand yard stare in a daze
As the flame comes into view I can't help but smile
Then, all at once, I'm feeling content for a while.

# Lady Serenity

I never thought I'd meet Serenity
For her I've grown such an affinity
She always seemed just beyond reach.
God knows this keeper is a peach.

The cross I carry is a heavy one.
Bearing such a weight isn't fun
This peace makes the load lighter
It makes me commit to being a fighter.

For years I've searched for this relief.
I've needed help dealing with some grief.
Serenity has always been an unseen goal
Now that we've met there's hope in my soul.

I found her in a place I never expected
This heaven I hope will never be regretted.
It helps that I'm being taught how to cope
From here I carry on maintaining hope.

Knowing peace makes me feel strange
However, this is a most welcome change
Now what must I do to live this way?
Is there a new devil I have to pay?

This blessing was more than Heaven sent
I can now fathom just what God meant.
I'm thankful to know such a feeling
Now I see why this state is so appealing.

# God Help Me

Months ago I muttered a very simple prayer
These three words, "God, help me," was all I could dare
At the time I had no clue to the prayer's magnitude.
The changes I incurred began with a new attitude.

I can say the prayer was answered, that's for sure
What was I hoping for — a miracle or even a cure?
So far I've received more than I bargained for
God's offered a chance to walk through a new door.

On the other side of the door is a world made new
It's not made easy or pain free that much is true.
Yet with a new way of thinking I am well armed
Cloaked in self-forgiveness for all those I've harmed.

My own eyes are halfway open to God's working hand
This is just a part of Him answering my demand
The unexplainable ways of Fate I can now explain
God is the mythical Fate I assumed only spreads pain.

His control is ultimate and totally unwavering
It's God's design under which I've been laboring
My false conviction of being in control is such a joke
Forcing my hand in self-will has left me broke.

The prayer's gone full circle but the work's just begun
Away from God's help I've tried so hard to run.
Yet I'm getting just what the simple prayer asked
Those three words, "God, help me," I dared speak at last.

# Deo Vindice

The world is seeking out a reason
Demanding answers for all my treason
My words falter trying to explain
Only meager logic behind the pain.

Tomorrow has blossomed into yesterday
Brilliant in trembling shades of gray
A bitter, cold dawn always on repeat
Burning dusk that's never complete.

Vindication burning in its splendor
A touch of forgiveness so tender
Amends are spoken that I adore
Among ears too afraid to ignore.

Sinister punishment is meted out
Here I'm a slave to my own doubt
It comes down to the flogging lash
Crippled by a life reduced to ash.

The savior points out my every flaw
Condemnation borne by history's law
While Fate decrees what she'll save,
My callused hands dig this grave.

Dying Past offers up a final sigh
The Future mourns for those who die
See the mason set another stone
Hearing the Present trying to atone.

# Dusk

I watch dusk as it kisses the sky
Choking down and stifling a cry
The colors they dance and waltz
Perfectly clear of any true faults.

It's bittersweet seeing the sun go
The moon it can never overthrow
Darkness comes and lights go on
Minutes creep along until dawn.

A halo of light embraces the city
This goes far beyond being pretty
The cars go by at such a pace
Surely Heaven's here in this place.

Is this when God's angels rest?
This day's end I love the best.
Peace descends upon the earth
Prayers ascend laden with worth.

Hustle and bustle goes on some more
Even when light takes the exit door.
Far too many have forsaken sleep
Forgetting their dreams once deep.

Night's entrance is known to annoy
Though some, the darkness they enjoy
So here's to the stars and the moon
They catch us here singing their tune.

# Eyes Turned Within

There's a darkness deep inside me
Even the blind men they can see
It's like a monster in its cage
Darker it gets with passing age.

Seldom is it kept at bay
It heeds not the words I say
Nothing holds it not even magic
Its end result is always tragic.

So easy, for it is running loose
And easily it can form a noose
The shadow it hesitates to be caught
Like a mythical dragon it is fought.

You see, the light it wages war
Peace is what we're fighting for
For the cause there is still no cry
But its either live free or die.

Weapons are useless on this field
Spartans return home on their shield
No Thermopolae or fabled last stand
Dark and Light fight by my hand.

The Darkness I used to so enjoy
Yet, its facilities I couldn't employ
The tide is unbalanced and turning
Resolution is coming, for it I'm yearning.

# How Many Devils

I can't face another devil
Living now on a different level
Familiar demons they play hard
Serenading like a medieval bard.

That existence ain't no joke
Take you and leaves you broke
I see this now in my hindsight
Like a blind man sees the light.

Back at square one I begin
Roll the dice to gamble on sin
Place your bet with a prayer
Take a risk wager on a dare.

Life is one big fat choice
She'll drown out every voice
Leaves you wondering what's next
There's no instruction book or text.

The angels they all seem to leave
Alone you'll learn how to grieve
What sane man asks for this?
A myth like the wedded bliss.

How many devils are left to pay?
Fighting to feel the sun's rays
I feel the heat pour over me
It's solution to the "Nth" degree.

# Light

Let me say the light becomes you
It looks better than the shadows
This is like the sweetest déjà vu
Living on Fiddler's Green's meadows

Can you feel the light's embrace?
It is like a blanket so warm
Feel peace now you've run the race
At your back recedes many a storm.

Life's sun has overtaken the moon
Blue sky replaces all the stars
I guess this didn't happen too soon
My new days are founded on scars.

Can you wait to live through tomorrow?
The future is bright to those who see.
Yesterday you thrived on your sorrow
These days the light sets you free.

Of hope I have more than enough
My reserves are no longer depleted
What happened yesterday sure was tough
You refuse to let light be defeated.

Hear the sound of the flying light
It crashes a lot like its thunder
The storms replaced by what might
You'll leave nothing torn asunder.

# Year Down

Oh, it's amazing what changes in a year
Things fade away that once were so dear
The first thing to become new is the clock
Every day and month is under key and lock

Tomorrow is impossible for anyone to predict
Time's inevitable passing is God's harsh verdict
No crystal ball awaits us to divulge its tales
Every hour's death is marked by chiming bells.

Everything I had then has gone and died
Yesteryear's bones in a barren crypt reside
Now in hindsight I can see all the clues
Had I listened I wouldn't have met the blues

Looking back I see how I wasn't close to right
There is a lot to be said for having hindsight
Nowadays everything tends to make sense
Yet the future still keeps me in suspense.

I'm working very hard to make a new start
The old life is almost too much for my heart
I refuse to keep doing this over and over again
Today I pay for yesterday's rampant sin.

Never could I have guessed about today
Last year was like a Texas storm in May
Where I'm at now is behind a waiting dawn
In the breadth of one year only evil is gone.

# Blessed By the Best

Boy, I love to count my blessings
Like eating Turkey with lots of dressing
I write them out like a Christmas list
Finding there's nothing God has missed.

Today I'm blessed for air in my lungs
And the fact that I'm still young
God works miracles in me and you
Like the promised rainbow this is true.

I'm blessed completely inside and out
My voice raises in a thankful shout
To my Father above goes all the praise
For He blesses me in countless ways.

This prodigal son has final come home
For twelve years, lost I did roam
I was a slave to a tempting old devil
Now in my blessings I chose to revel.

I'm blessed for tomorrow and yesterday
The past and the future they don't hold sway
If today's all I got I'll give it my best
I am Job, the ace of Satan's many tests.

God has shown me that I am dear
He's painting a portrait that is so clear
I'm saved by the water on the Jordan's banks
So, I count these blessings and give thanks.

# God is a Gentleman

When I was using dope I didn't think of God
It was like His existence I had outlawed.
He was merely a spectator to how I chose to live
A Being whose power was to only take or to give.

I crumpled up God and cast Him to the side
The relationship we once had I effortlessly denied
Any hope for my life very quickly became extinct
Without knowing God my existence was made succinct.

Being free of God immediately opened a void
So I relied on love and the drugs I so enjoyed.
I figured the drugs would work much faster
They dulled the pain from not being my own master.

My God stepped aside to wait just like a gentleman
Up His sleeve was his "Ace" known as His Plan.
He bided his time while I made everything a mockery
I insulted His grace and reveled in debauchery.

When the time is right God will re-enter the picture
I have faith in this because of written scripture
It's up to me to invite Him back into my life
Before I jump from the heights in a final dive.

I'm not sure how this relationship is going to work
Every time I pushed God away I felt like a jerk.
Maybe when I trust Him things will come as they should
Together the two of us can build something good.

# *Relapse*

# Dreams Set to Repeat

There I was clawing my way down a familiar street
Why was I dreaming of another repeating defeat?
No matter what I did I couldn't even stay awake
That's when I learned dreams are very hard to fake.


It has been weeks since the last time I dreamed
From my old thinking I figured I was redeemed
Why now, what triggered my new nighttime thinking?
Between the "how" and the "why" there's nothing linking.


Perhaps this was a reminder of what was yesterday
I was heavily bombarded as in my bunk I did lay
Never did I ask God for this new type of reverie
Yet this time around I don't claim this a tragedy.


The people in this dream I didn't want to see again
As if those folks had to remind me of every old sin
Was this a punishment? No! I refuse to believe so
This was just a journey to before I hit my true low.


Funny how everything in the dream seemed to go right
It was as if the bad had been removed from my sight
Sunlight consumed a sky that was once painted black
Reality appeared with the dawn and the world came back.


Upon waking up I found I'd never felt so very glad
Briefly as a thought did I feel kind of darkly sad
Like the clock and time this dream will only fade
Now in peace the memories can rest as they've been paid.

# Deeply Consumed

The pain is deep within my aching abused gut
Its gaping mouth is the one I can't shut.
God help me, the hurt is getting to be bad
It makes me want to cry because I'm so mad.

This blackness settles deep inside of me
Everything is blocked out so I can't see
My stomach churns as it does a backflip
I'm traveling on some kind of bad acid trip.

To my chest the hurt spreads like a cancer
I turn to God hoping for some kind of answer
The air in my lungs is being squeezed out
Let me go from these arms withered in doubt.

My heart shudders but not with any delight
This time it beats to the tune of severe fright
The pumping blood has given up and gone cold
Where's the refuge now my soul has been sold?

Pain, it flows to and from every inch of my body
God knows it makes me feel so damn shoddy
Can I run from myself this time around?
My fleeing figure can't even make a sound.

Embrace me, dead, evil, fearful, malignant pain
You're pouring down like a hurricane's rain
Draping me in funeral black laced in disdain
Leading me on a leash back to being insane.

# Hell's Maze

I'm lost but I can't cry out for any aid
Somewhere I went off the path that was laid
Now I'm surrounded by the unknown and I'm afraid.

There are no signs left to point out the way to go
Which direction to take is what I don't know
I'm here at the bottom because I stooped so low.

Hansel and Gretel's bread crumbs have been swept away
Without the trail to guide me my hope begins to fray
I hope to God I'll make it to another day.

The sun is sinking fast and time is running out
My chances of survival I can't help but to doubt
Yet my voice is shot and I can't lift a shout.

I've been crawling in the mud on torn up knees
Looking like a blind man unsure of what he sees
I'm a tattered flag unraveling in a heavy breeze.

Trying to find my way home has been a form of hell
This journey is memorable but it's impossible to tell
But much like you, I'm not sure if this ends well.

There's no hand outstretched for me to grab hold
I've run out of options and everything dear was sold
I'll stagger and crawl through this maze 'til I'm old.

# "Relapse"

It's funny how nothing's changed
I'm still me, I'm still so deranged
My mind doesn't work like yours
Trust me we fight different wars

A broken record won't stop spinning
Playing a tune reserved for sinning
Over and over again, it won't stop
The masses dance on until they drop

Nothing's changed; watch me break
I don't care about what's at stake
Yes, I think my "give a shit" is gone
It ran away along with beloved dawn

Bad decisions seem to be my cross
Why? That riddle leaves me at a loss
Sing the same song; different verse
I accept I am my own hated curse

Now fault me if you will, I don't care
I'm far beyond the hope of a prayer
You can hate but never understand
Go ahead and draw a line in the sand

Words will only fall on deafened ears
Fables can't warm my heart's fears
Waste your time playing my savior
Many have failed to fix my behavior

"I'm fixed!" Became another bold lie
My laughter never had time to die
I faked out the most educated fools
Hell yeah I used them like work tools

How sick I feel not an ounce of pain
It's too easy to embrace the insane
Regret? Remorse? I know them not
At least while I load a narcotic shot

Truly I know I fooled myself mostly
An obvious truth I guard so closely
At least I accept what I have done
From this monster I refuse to run

Roll a dollar bill as I crush up a pill
God, but how I've missed this thrill
The spoon is tarnished and so burnt
It holds such a euphoric old current

Who's shocked that change failed?
Not me, not you, the truth is veiled
Deep inside I knew I'd be here again
Guess what? I fucking love this sin

Don't pray for me now or tomorrow
God's loans are the worst to borrow
I don't want your love or your heart
Either one I will so easily tear apart

My soul refuses to acknowledge you
I'm so wrong, damn right that's true
Maybe, my being broken gets me off
That's so bad it causes you to scoff

Derision feeds relapse's hot flames
I know the rules to addictions games
Like me they are broken with ease
Another dictator you can't appease

Shame on me for stating a falsehood
That's why nothing went as it should
Shame on you for you believed in me
The next let down you'll get for free

I completed my chase of getting high
This relapse I enjoyed safely, no lie
Next time I'm sure it will get harder
I'll end up being my very own martyr

# "Why, Jay?"

I suppose I owe you an explanation
All I want from this is my salvation.
In my mind the reasons and excuses
None are able to explain my bruises.

The storm on the horizon I did see
Indifference spelt out doom for me.
I turned my back and prayed for rain
In waiting I sowed my crops of pain.

I wanted a last dance with the devil.
I know what awaits and in it I revel.
He dances like a legless, junkie fiend
But he left me feeling so demeaned.

I did what I did based on my instinct
Forgetting the past made it extinct
Understand this disease is purely bad
Living close to it can drive one mad.

It was worse than it was long before
Another battle lost in an unending war.
I can't lie so I offer up nothing in reply,
My explanation is lost in a weary sigh.

# My Last Masquerade

I never took a chance on stealing a second glance
Plunged right ahead in this masquerade for the dead
Where mortality is shed with every chaotic dance.

The music plays a dirge causing my skeleton to emerge
Decorations so dark keep me from hitting my mark
Corrupted dead waltz in the park to their every urge.

Guests show and tell amidst this crowd from Hell
Distinguished Death floats on the floor stealing breath
He finds nothing left to rob from flesh turned pale.

I mingle in the crowd of spirits bereft of the proud
Groups of damned souls are under an unseen control
The broken are made whole as the music grows loud.

No laughter emits nor are parlor games played
This dead man's ball is my pride before the fall
The phantoms roam every hall after admittance is paid.

There's no light, yet it's so damn dark it's bright
As I walk along I trip over the cavernous canyon's lip
Nothing exists to catch my grip before I fall from sight.

I think I'll give in and dance with my waiting sin
My cold clammy hand stretches in a pleading demand
This foray was not planned so I'll never attend again.

# "The Day After..."

I stand up again and wipe off the dust
Something still shines beneath the rust
That was nothing more than a bad choice
Failure on me to hear God's sweet voice

I won't bitch, I won't cry, I won't moan
Yes, the responsibility falls on me alone
Now I appreciate the good I know I can do
I understand God wanting to see me through

No, it didn't happen as if done by magic
Dare I say the outcome was not so tragic?
I got lucky, more so than I truly deserve
It took more pain to finally pierce a nerve

Nothing had changed except the tone of pride
I poked the monster that is too big to hide
There is no excuse therefore there's no reason
I won't attempt to justify this new treason

Let's leave this behind so I can move along
This time around let's dance to a new song
Don't let me pick the tune or start the dance
I'm able to admit I will blow every chance

I'm a drug addict in a most unnatural place
Sobriety is scary to me like a Demon's face
I don't need a reason to get high like others
Suffice it say that this life ain't my druthers

Don't ask why because I haven't a clear answer
Now you can see that addiction is my cancer
I'll beat myself up worse than you ever could
But why bother when I can focus on the good?

# Pretty Presages

The coldest shiver is crawling down my spine
While in Earth's boiling sand I draw a line
I know this feeling inside my gut all too well
It presages an unpleasant decent down to Hell.

At some point I made a choice to stand
With no clear thought as to life's demands
Now I feel like my back is up against a wall
That presages a long way down will I fall.

I have an ability to make some real bad choices
Unfortunately I can't lie and say I hear voices
What I've done has long been termed wrong
That presages the melody of a sad, sad song.

See, I get these feelings that hurt or burn
Sometimes it even hurts enough I might learn.
More often than not I shrug and keep going
That action presages an awful lot of groaning.

Good Lord above, do you see how I live?
I'm pretty sure I've been leaking like a sieve.
There's a lot I have to do just to rally
That presages numbers added to my tally.

# Satan's Roller Coaster

I'm stuck on this Satan's roller coaster ride
A long time ago the kill switch went and died.
My stomach's in knots from the ups and downs
Everything is spinning as I go round and round.

With every year I live, the speed goes higher
I fear the car's attached by only a thin wire
Disembarking is nowhere near a lucky option
Every turn on this ride puts my sanity for adoption.

The operator cackles on with his maniacal glee
He gets off on the knowledge that I'm not free
My cries for help he continues to ignore
This character of evil I'm so wrong to implore.

Vomit rises in my throat and chokes away my air
No words form in my mouth to sound any prayer
Mouth open wide I try to scream to my savior
But I'm forsaken here by my ungodly behavior.

The wind in my face stings like a thousand pins
My expression is frozen in a grimacing grin
Every inch of track is memorized in my fear
How do I live knowing the end is nowhere near?

Unknown forces push me down onto this hard seat
Resisting is impossible for I'm too far gone and beat
I'm crushed by the weights of my dark, dead past
I don't care anymore how long this hell will last.

# Something Evil Comes

Something dark and evil on the horizon does loom
The cheery sky above is being cast into gloom
I'm afraid my anxiety is running out of room
While the bleakness ahead is spelling my doom.

I'll get to pay the Pied Piper pretty soon
Then for a time unknown I'll dance this tune
The song he plays turns a man into a lune
Dance, dance, dance until exhausted I swoon.

The coming storm flashes and booms in the sky
I know I can't escape so I won't even try.
To the shelter, like a bird, I hurry and fly
I brace for impact as the storm goes by.

When the storm hits it's like a wave on a wall
The flood is overpowering and the bricks will fall
As I flail in swirling waters it's for help I call
Desperate efforts and sandbags won't help at all.

The eye of the storm passes by much too fast
I savor the brief peace I know won't last
While my ship sinks I cling to the broken mast
Waiting for the storm to resume, praying it will pass.

In the end the clouds break apart and disappear
Every time the storm rages I'm embraced by fear
I forget the tempest fades and peace is near
Among the wreckage and debris I still stand here.

# Knocking at My Door

I can hear evil knocking at my door
The Devil waits hoping to even the score
I've answered the summons before
O'l Scratch on the porch crying for more

To buy time I cut off the worn doorbell
I locked myself inside my own jail
Outside the Devil took my world to hell
How lucky that I have this story to tell.

On the porch he waits biding his time
Did some demonic informer drop a dime?
With Lucifer's punishment for my crime
There's no bodies left to dissolve in lime.

Still he knocks trying to collect his due
There's no such thing as a lie that's true
I can't wait this out, he'll never be through.
Evil's the last thing you want to screw.

The door splinters and the hinges crack
False protection has fallen under attack
Against me I know the odd's stacked
All I want is my soul to come back.

The door will fall onto my barricade
I hope by then evil will be dismayed
Some say to give up what must be paid
Yet I embrace the sacrifice God laid.

# Imperfect Mistake

I'll be your perfectly imperfect mistake
Around you I will never try to be fake
Why not set us up for this flaming fall?
I'll be here at your every beck and call.


All I can say now is this, "As you so wish"
You got me feeling like I'm a hooked fish
What I can make you is this one promise
I'll always be the one man you'll miss.


I'll be your only, first, final, fatal dance
Such is the risk of chasing true romance
We'll reel and waltz past the fading moon
From our high we'll be coming down soon.


Take a risk if you are feeling so brave
Let us be what the other will try to save
But I will be your heroin's favored rush
You'll feel me every single time you blush.


I'll be the last long step that sends you down
We can learn what it really means to frown
Together we can laugh in the moon's light
Let us become blinded by the other's sight.


What's left to say but this, "Come with me"
Which of us is the slave and which one is free?
Let me let you drive me far beyond insane
How can I repay you without causing any pain?

# *The Final Battle*

# Death's Finality

The silence of the dead rings loud
Ashen faces behind Death's shroud
Above us life lingers in each soul
What man of us claims any control?

We fight the good fight and true
Yet hesitate when Death comes for you
Terminal life always meets an end
Our spirits to Heaven the angels send.

No one can run or truly hide
It's mortality always at our side
Be it by Fate or a lottery's draw
From Life's stage we bow and withdraw.

Our own allotted time is a curse
If we live looking for our hearse.
Seize the day and take every chance
Don't be left alone at the last dance.

One day your heart will beat its last
To memories loved one hold fast
Will you look down from up above
Please fill our hearts with love.

There's lessons all must teach
If we keep happiness within reach
I know we will meet again
It's no question of if, but when.

# Falling

I'm falling through the heavens of sorrow
Passing beyond the valleys of tomorrow.
Will I land beyond the time I borrow?

Shadows envelope me as I continually fall
I'm like a plane plummeting after a stall.
My voice dies out the louder I call.

Faster the clouds pass me as I roar by
The sky's blue embrace is really a lie.
Pastures below me will pad me as I die.

I am racing to catch my thorny crown.
No warmth in the atmosphere to slow me down.
The oxygen is thin enough to make one drown.

Gravity pulls down the cold stratosphere
Upon Atlas' shoulders burdens rest near
Between the two vanishes what was once dear.

The weightlessness leaves a strange feeling
My fall's end result has left me here reeling
Nothing could have stopped me from healing.

Darkness consumes my once clearest foresight
Nothing will remain from Heaven's light
The outcome below me seems right.

# Alamo

Here I stand on the walls of this self-made Alamo
I think the ending of that story is one we all know
History tells me I can't surrender, so here I stay
Hoping for the best while keeping the enemy at bay.

On the horizon snaps a banner bathed in red
No mercy and no quarter tends to go as unsaid
Outmanned and outgunned by a blood thirsty horde
I'm accepting the hard truth I'll die by the sword.

I've called for help more times than I can count
Now comes doubt about the defense I will mount.
Aid is coming soon but it's nowhere near enough
It's obvious the coming fight is going to be tough.

The day is looming when I'll face a line in the sand
What's etched in the ground is a hellish demand.
Stay to die or run to live will be the final choice
It's not an answer to be given by any mortal voice.

When they attack I know my walls they will breach
Holding the enemy back is an option out of reach
All I can do is fall back and fight room by room
Paying no mind to the inevitable and final doom.

Never again will I leave these walls behind me
I'm a slave to this place and will never be free
My body they'll place on a pyre and light the fuse
The final insult for fighting a battle deemed to lose.

# The Road Always Traveled

Time is merely a winding ribbon of road
Crumbling under a burdensome load
Through mountains and woods it goes
Where it'll end nobody really knows.

This route is one everyone will travel
Behind us the ribbon begins to unravel
What lies ahead is kept within a shadow
Step by step we mark past time's meadows.

The pavement is marred by bumps and holes
Every obstruction plays pre-destined roles
No one person's path is completely smooth
After walking a while we get into a groove.

Time's road isn't always traveled alone
Next to each of us footsteps are shown
Was it God who played the road builder?
Asphalt and tar the tools of the wielder.

This route is forever strong and well paved.
To complete this journey may make one saved
Years and days pass away at the roadside
Minutes and seconds have tried so hard to hide.

There's no exits anywhere before the end
Until Death you walk on trying to mend
Time's road is not unlike Fate's highway
Both are paved in shades of gray.

# Final Fatal Fix

Once more I tie on a tourniquet
Asking God, "Why can't I quit?"
I know I'm tired of this shit
When will I take my final hit?

Veins lay blown out below the skin
There goes the needle and blood again
I let go and release the belt
Feel my body as it starts to melt

I fight as my eyes begin to close
Am I sinking into Death's throes?
This time I've bought the farm
Only I have caused myself this harm.

This poison for so long I craved
Pushing myself far beyond saved
The demons are holding a reception
Craftily adorned by their deception

Yes, I have served the wrong God
Addicted to a life that's outlawed
Now I want to come back to life
I must stop walking the edge of a knife.

Sure, this dragon I have tried to slay
I've been fighting night and day
No one gets away before they pay
This battle has led me far astray.

# Remain

Why do I remain on this earth?
Compared to some I've little worth
Yet, they are gone and here I am
Willing to be a sacrificial lamb.

God's plan is man's great mystery
None of us claim to have mastery
Some say the answers are in a book
Through the pages I've tried to look.

I've done nothing I labeled as great
By thirty I thought I'd meet my fate
There must be things still in store
Something remains for me to live for.

I've seen so many pass in a hearse
Is being left behind a kind of curse
How many flowers placed at a grave?
Wishing the deceased I could save.

No hero or martyr can I ever be
When my own flaws are too easy to see
God expects me to carry this cross
While condoling with other folk's loss

Why do I remain still in this place?
So close, so far from God's face
His answer I have sought to hear
As I wipe away a forlorn tear.

# Internal Strife

God and Satan wage their wars inside of me
On the frontlines I stand a willing draftee
Back and forth the angels and demons spill blood
Celestial life forces are spilt in the mud.

The dark has held sway in besieging the light
Like the Alamo of Texas it's a one way fight
I've sent pleas for help to deafened ears
Who's left that's willing to fight these fears?

Where are the heaven's battalions and bayonets?
Still they are fighting a rear guard of regrets.
Darkness closes in like the Nazis of Thirty-nine
I think the angels cannot cross over the Rhine.

I've been fighting so long it feels like forever
Vaguely I recall God's promise to win each endeavor.
Don't tell me how it's darkest before dawn
That's a line in the sand that's long been drawn.

I'm stuck in the midst of a war of attrition
Which side lies about sanctity of the mission?
There's no way out that is safe and sound
Retreat is an option better left unfound.

It looks like Hell comes in a wave attack
Phantom-faced demons ensconced in black.
My ammunition is gone leaving hands or blade
The call of charge sounds a refusal to fade.

The lines clash and I look away in pain.
Bodies in combat begin falling like rain.
This battle is not what I bargained for
I'd hate to encounter this struggle's encore.

God and the devil are my Lee and Grant
This war is a long forgotten Rembrandt.
My reserves are gone and tragically spent.
Where's my relief, a needed supplement?

# Mortal

Why does God take one and leave another?
A Mom, a Dad, a Sister, a Brother?
He takes someone we love the most
Leaving us haunted by their ghost.

Where's the rhyme or the reason?
Does this come and go by the season?
The widows search to know God's "why"
Motherless children are left to cry.

We blame God through our anger
Asking why he took not a stranger.
We fail to hear his heart break
Not seeing this was for their sake.

To all Death comes and Death goes
That's the way that every life flows.
From it no mortal can run and hide
If you say otherwise then you've lied.

The Pied Piper demands what is due
A mortal soul is a payment true.
We each owe the very same debt
Yet against Death no man will bet.

Don't you dare let hope fade away,
Banished to a limbo painted gray.
I believe we will all meet again —
No matter how hefty our own sin.

# Last Dance

It all started with a song's haunting melody
What happened after the chorus isn't a parody.
I stopped in my tracks to try and catch my breath
Felt like I had just done a huge shot of meth.

There we were again and she expected one dance
That night I was too far gone to spare a glance.
This song just reminded me of one special night
Then the memory fled leaving me full of fright.

I stood like a frozen fool unable to even twitch
Angrily I glared at the radio that evil bitch.
Ghosts flowed around me along with the song
The wish that came next I knew to be wrong.

"Please God, one more night and I'll do my best.
No matter what happens I'll put the past to rest."
A desperate bid and the plea was sent by prayer
What right have I to ask? It just wasn't fair.

Another night came back all with a giant rush
Vividly I recall even the tone of her blush
Here the memory stays cluttering my mind
I have it hidden in a place only I can find.

If I got just one last night to live again,
I'd make God proud and I'd face my sin
The opportunity seemed to be at my fingertips
But yet again I bumbled and let it slip.

Of course, I didn't go back for one last try
God doesn't work that way and I wonder why
I hoped this time he'd make an exception
Truly I was looking to make another deception.

It begs to be asked would I have done differently.
There's no answer to give that is true completely
All I can say is that I truly hope so
Yet in the end, its God, not me, who knows.

A portion of the proceeds from this book will be used to support the work of the Freedom Court. If you would like to make a personal contribution to the Freedom Court, contact

Mike Stevens
2407 82nd Street
Lubbock, TX  79423

CPSIA information can be obtained
at www.ICGtesting.com
Printed in the USA
LVHW020216230419
615088LV00014B/308/P